Praise fo

"These are stories of strength, survival, love, transformation and triumph. She has her readers sitting beside her as she humbly learns to be a mentor with the youth. She offers that the need for control must be put aside, and instead asks questions and offers exercises to help young people move from behaviors that keep them stuck in self-destructive behaviors into leadership roles where they themselves become the next generation of mentors for younger children."

>—Elsie Dennis, Shuswap, Former Communications Consultant for the Episcopal Native American and Indigenous Ministries, Bishop's Committee at St. Mathew/San Mateo in Auburn, WA.

"*Stamp It Holy* teaches and inspires through its storytelling. The stories center on the transformation of familial and societal pain into the practice of choosing to see possibilities for alternative lessons different from the usual messages of feeling unworthy and trapped. Author Kaze Gadway says in the book, "Every spiritual journey begins with the understanding of being cherished unconditionally." After reading this book, I find myself reflecting often on the power of deep listening and inviting the youth to remember things that have worked in their lives. The stories in this book celebrate the power to heal ourselves by tapping into the power to transform our narratives. Aloha"

>—Lelanda Lee, Episcopal lay leader in Longmont, Colorado, active in social justice work as an Anti-Racism Trainer, ABCD (Asset Based Community Development) Advocate, and Christian Formation Catechist.

"In seeing, tasting, and laughing the holy takes courage. With survival-mode a blanket, a broken heart, home, or community can be the ultimate battleground for God's peace. This is a manual for that, or any kind of youth ministry."

>—Ronald R. Braman, Eastern Shoshone Tribe, Wind River Reservation. Youth & Music Minister Fort Hall Indian Reservation.

"Awesome stories. You write about those times when we struggled to be more. Reading these stories about our journey pulls me back to be Native Strong. Finding the Holy in hard places like Skid Road or in the midst of drama makes the effort worth it. I will read this book again and again."

—Jay Begay, a Dine youth

"The book is a map of the journey we have all taken from the dark place to one of healing. Letting us tell the deep traditional stories of our grandmothers fills me with honor. I am now reading the stories to my young children that they may also have hope."

—Katy Yazee, Dine and Ute youth

"This book is a window into lives most of us rarely, if ever encounter. To be able to learn about these youths' concerns and cares through Kaze Gadway's powerful lens of attempting holy listening adds an even more powerful witness. These are voices we need to hear and attempt to hear better. To listen and to be present to how each of us has a gift to give and how to help unlock it is a gift in itself. May this group of stories enliven and invigorate your desire to go forth and continue to make all we see holy."

—Katherine Córdova, SCHC Community activist

STAMP IT HOLY

STAMP IT HOLY

STORIES AND WISDOM OF NATIVE YOUTH

KAZE GADWAY

ALBUQUERQUE, NEW MEXICO

DEDICATION

I dedicate this book to the youth who traveled on this journey as the Spirit Journey Youth. We took time for serious and fun stuff. We made mistakes together and forgave each other. We learned how to be generous as we cared for those who live fragile lives. They blessed me with their spirituality and insights. We healed each other.

ACKNOWLEDGMENTS

Many people made this journey possible. I can't name them all. Some spent time with youth face to face, encouraging them to reach high in their expectations. Some became their heroes. Some welcomed them into their homes and hearts. Some provided funds. Some contacted them through social media.

The Rev. Dorothy Saucedo (Dine Elder) and the Rev. Vivian Winter Chaser (Lakota Elder), deacons in the Episcopal Church shine as influential models of Native beauty and leadership..

Bishop Steven Charleston and Bishop Carol Gallagher (Native Episcopal Bishops) gave them words to live by.

Bishop Kirk Smith and Bishop Michael Vono baptized and confirmed them, honoring their Native spirituality. Bishop Mary Douglas Glasspool spent time with us on our mission trips to Skid Road and asking relevant questions. Bishop Daniel G.P. Gutierrez did training in our leadership group.

Kelli Grace Kurtz, Ann Johnson, Earl Gibson, Francis Cantella, Doug Bleyle, Richard Valantasis, Timothy Dombek, Jennifer Phillips, Pamela Mullac, Norman Burke, Scott Hankins, Barrett Van Buren and Annette Joseph welcomed them as Episcopal Priests in their congregations. The late Rev. Terry Star guided them in his ministry.

John Benge, Michael McNew, Phyllis Phelps, Sue and Kurt Stetzer, Steve Darden, Jana Milhon-Martin, David and Alice Packard, Kathleen Head, and Kathleen O'Leary took time to talk and do activities with them.

To protect their privacy, Leonard Kohout digitally disguised the faces of the youth.

Priscilla H. Wilson supported this group from the beginning as well as editing each story.

There are so many more that did something special to affirm these youth as cherished people. You live in our hearts. A special shout out to the congregations at St. John's in LaVerne, California and St. John's in Williams, Arizona for their continuous welcome and support.

Stamp It Holy Copyright © 2017 by Kaze Gadway.

All rights reserved. Printed in the United States of America. No part of this book may be used or reproduced in any manner without written permission exception in the case of reprints in the context of reviews.

TeamTech Press
8101 Mission Road, Prairie Village, KS 66208
Pris@TeamTechPress.com

www.teamtechpress.com

ISBN: 978-0-692-84679-7

Library of Congress Control Number: 2017934305

Cover and text designed by Tim Lynch

TABLE OF CONTENTS

FOUNDATIONAL PATTERNS OF YOUTH GROUP 13
    Beginnings 13
    Defining Moments 16

SECTION ONE:
CHANGING IMAGES TO PROMOTE GROWTH 25
    Goodness in Life 31
    Past as Treasure 41
    Future as Open 50
    Self as Valued 56
    NATALIE: Self-Image of Strength 66

SECTION TWO:
RECLAIMING STORIES TO RESTORE DIGNITY 69
    Managing Issues 73
    Affirming Life 86
    Expanding Scope 95
    ROB: Story of Managing for Himself. 107

SECTION THREE:
SACRED PATHS TO GIVE MEANING 111
    Awakening 115
    Wonder 123
    Compassion 134
    Blessing 141
    TOBY: Path of Holiness 149

APPENDIX
ADDITIONAL CURRICULUM FROM
YOUTH GROUP 153
    Section One: Curriculum for Social Environment 154
    Section Two: Curriculum for Spiritual Domain 160

"Listen, however it comes to you, listen wherever you are, and you will hear the sacred speak, a language born before time, a meaning meant for you."

—The Right Reverend Steven Charleston, Choctaw elder and Episcopal Bishop

Skid Road, L.A.

"*I believe in the Great Spirit, the creator of all living people; of that which flies or crawls or swims; of all growing things, and of all that makes up the earth and the seas. I believe in the one who is beyond me yet continues to cherish me in spite of what I do.*"

Creed of Spirit Journey Youth, 2012

FOUNDATIONAL PATTERNS OF YOUTH GROUP

Beginnings

Brown eyes and dark faces look at the table, the windows or the wall—in every direction except toward me. We gather in a small church room in Winslow, Arizona, in the year 2000 to form a youth group. I clear my throat, clutching my papers filled with ice breakers and helpful hints on well-known group procedures. Seven teenagers squirm like puppies as I talk.

I stand up looking around at the group. "This doesn't work, does it?" A few nod their heads. We move to the back yard and sit on the grass. "Let's go around the circle and say one word on something you feel grateful about." My voice cracks a little.

We wait in silence between each response as the teenagers call out their words, "family," "friends," "guitar," and "pizza." Dave looks down as he calls out "staying alive." He starts weaving grass stems together.

I search for another question. "How about praying for strength to face one thing we are afraid of?" I ask, not expecting much. "Maybe it will put things in focus for us."

Ernie stutters. "I'm scared to go home."

Stunned, I look at the others as they all nod. They understand opening a door and not knowing if someone wasted or strung out will greet them with a fist. Others begin sharing on a deeper level than I expected. "How do I deal with my father when he returns from prison?" "Teachers don't get it that I have to skip school sometimes to babysit my younger sister when she is sick." "Why do people hate us Natives?"

We close by talking about what we want in future meetings. Suggestions include more discussion among themselves, fun activities in which they can relax, and more silence in which they can think. I feel unsure about my ability to offer the fluidity they need. I realize that when they raise a question, they do not want to wait until Sunday to formally examine the issue. They want a response **now**.

Our next meeting takes place Wednesday after school in the play yard. From then on, meetings happen whenever two or three of us find each other. Sometimes I see a group of kids in a back yard or at a fast food place.

Dave brings some sage to one of the meetings. "Can we burn this? It makes me feel at home." We light the sage and add other sacred practices from both Native and Christian traditions. Our agenda stays flexible and open ended which lets us see holiness in unexpected encounters. Sometimes blessing the space by placing cornmeal in the four sacred directions opens our minds to startling insights.

This cements our future discussions. Coping with experiences rather than discussing creeds or beliefs revitalizes us. We swim upstream in order to go beyond survival in this vulnerable population. We fortify our identity in something more than the existing lethal atmosphere of a border town like Holbrook or Winslow.

In the early years we barely hold together as we encounter the constant barrage of poverty, addiction and violence. Listening to the police scream at us for no other reason than our being gathered as a group in a parking lot terrifies us. I wonder if wiping blood off their faces, finding places to hide from drama or stepping around hung over bodies will always be the daily routine. Will I always find police or gang bangers at their door when I collect them for meetings? What shapes their lives but unrelenting catastrophes?

Before I succumb to the prevailing hopelessness, a larger picture emerges. The youth have memories of ancient stories being shared by a caring grandmother. These revolve around the kinship of all creation, all things on Mother Earth and Father Sky. This understanding becomes the bedrock of Native pride—we are all relatives.

"Natives don't do this. Know your kin. Show respect," represents common grandmotherly wisdom to deal with bullying or disrespect toward elders. Their traditional stories illustrate how to live in beauty and harmony.

As I gain their trust I discover that most of their families pray daily to the Great Spirit, the Creator of all. Sometimes they pray with corn pollen, or tobacco, or sage. In these ceremonies they give thanks to the kinship of all in Mother Earth and Father Sky, including strangers and frogs and trees. Traditional practices surface whenever endless wretchedness appears. Spiritual foundations lie deep in the DNA of the Native community. A young Hopi teen waves at an area in the distance. "We have prayer sticks there by the waterholes. My family has prayed there for centuries." Everyone ran toward the van when it started raining until Les says "It's a female rain. Enjoy it while it lasts." Youth laugh and stop running. I discover that 'female rain' is gentle without storms. Casual comments like these reveals their perception of the sacred in commonplace things.

A pattern emerges: this complex journey promises to be filled with profound concerns and refreshing surprises. We name ourselves Spirit Journey Youth as we explore walking in the two worlds of the Anglo culture and indigenous tradition.

My role as youth mentor keeps evolving. I want to alleviate their suffering. Yet the option of giving money or building houses remains unfeasible. What we can do together is to objectify the mess we find ourselves in and collectively expand our capacity to see the holy. Underneath everything, I want healing to take place. I want them to see goodness in themselves and their circumstances and reconcile with whatever terrifies them.

In the first few years, we organize mission trips to various places to see vulnerable people beyond their own home towns. In 2004 we propose a mission trip to Los Angeles Skid Road. As we walk around tents and pallets on the sidewalk, we feel the enormity of poverty. As we sit down on benches we talk about our discomfort in walking the Skid Row streets with wasted bodies everywhere or trying to eat lunch with hungry people. "What if they grab our food and run or they fight us?" Warily we plan to venture forth with several sack lunches per person. As we walk the streets clutching our brown bags, something profound happens. Our moods inexplicably lighten. Anxiety disappears. We begin joking and calling out greetings. We sit on benches and share our lunches with those around us. When we arrive at the van to depart, Rob says, "I don't want to leave. This has been awesome. I feel different."

I look around at the kids in their usual second hand clothing and bad haircuts. We stand around the van with only a few homeless people looking at us. "How can we mark it as holy?"

Toby stamps his foot down. "I stamp you holy," he cries out. We all follow suit and stamp the ground. After that, we stamp holy our profound encounters. It sets the tone for our common journey. It becomes our story.

Defining Moments

Certain turning points in our journey shaped us: inviting the disenfranchised to be in the group, taking trips to show alternative options in living, focusing on homelessness as our purpose, making Skid Road our symbol of sharing, incorporating Native traditions, participating in liturgical practices in different Churches, directing a youth center, and job training.

How did I get involved? My turning point began in 1990. I turned fifty after spending thirty years with global indigenous cultures on the staff of the Ecumenical Institute of Chicago. I taught, facilitated and implemented fourteen village economic and social projects in developing nations. To recapture my paternal Native heritage and continue living in indigenous communities, I moved to Arizona. After living and working on three reservations as a tribal employee in programs and planning I settled in Northern Arizona in 2000. There the Episcopal Diocese invited me to form a youth group. The congregations assured me "It will only be an hour each week."

"I can do that." I smile with confidence.

My one hour a week expands rapidly. Seven young people form the initial group. Six drop out for various reasons. One Native youth remains. He asks, "Can I bring my cousins who have lost their way?" The cousins bring several more relatives and close friends, some straight from juvenile detention. Their parents don't attend church. Most of the new members come from violence and poverty. Soon the juvenile probation officers allow the attendance at youth group to count as "community service." Now at the end of each meeting I motion with my hand. "Please pass in your probation papers." We laugh as almost everyone hands me a paper to sign.

Since I have spent my previous career being saturated by village issues, it seemed normal for me to respond to calls for rides to the hospital or to work through violent encounters.

After struggling a few years with the youth, the Episcopal Bishop of Arizona, Kirk Smith, assigns me as the youth missioner. I remain for thirteen years as their mentor. When I retired at seventy-three, I realized that I rarely slept all night. It had not been what I expected. I had been captured and delighted by a tradition filled with pain and blessings.

Our group expands over the years to include those who live in broken-down cars and in the alleyways. Some churches in town ask teens in trouble to stop attending their services so they join us. We get a reputation for welcoming anyone who walks in the door. A mother stops by our group meeting in Winslow to ask if her son can join. "We don't go to church and my son has really messed up in school." Mandy speaks for the group. "We don't ask questions and we don't have requirements." The kids clap. The mother looks startled but waves goodbye.

Toby says "I feel good about that. My family asks me what kind of group I've joined and now I can tell him. We talk about where our journey takes us when we welcome those who do not feel welcomed elsewhere.

As we struggle to define ourselves we take trips as often as possible. One weekend, we have a retreat in Fort Defiance (on the Navajo reservation) with other Natives. On the way back a young man leans over my shoulder as I am driving. "Listen, a girl asks that we pray for her."

"Okay," I reply. "Did she say why?"

"No!"

I think about this and then notice that the van full of kids has turned silent.

"Do you mean now?" I say as I clutch the wheel tighter.

"Yes."

I resist closing my eyes while driving seventy-five miles an hour. I pray for someone I don't know about something I know nothing about. Silence lasts for a long time after the prayer.

Then the questions start. "Why do others think that we are so bad?" "Why is there so much poverty among us?" "Are we really so different?" We have one of the best youth meetings ever driving along the interstate. It becomes a landmark for the type of eclectic meeting that works for us.

In-between our open forums, we take short and long trips. Sometimes we visit churches or national parks or just take long hikes. Each time, taking them away from the confinement of small town opinions exposes them to possibilities. Leaving our hometown even for short distances releases unexpected vitality and tolerance for a crowded van.

Then we begin long mission trips, west toward California and east toward Missouri. Our focus changes to serve the homeless rather than just getting away. Our mission concentrates on the most vulnerable. This emphasis touches their spiritual dimension. "My grandmother told me that we never turn away someone who needs food no matter how little we have," says one of the youth. Everyone nods.

Once we walk into a fast food place to eat in Colorado and a skinny white woman runs up to us. Some drug has turned her hyper. She can't stop moving around with jerky motions. "You got to help me," she says. "I need a hit or I will explode."

Without any hesitation, the junior high kids empty their pockets to give her their change. I want to protest that we should not help this person. I say nothing.

Later we talk about it. "You told us that it is not up to us to judge; God alone can judge," says Wayne.

"That's true," I admit. "Maybe she needs your generosity to know that if she survives, someone cares." Natalie gives a thumb up while the kids laugh.

Something changes us as we interact with street people, some of whom are close relatives. Almost all of our youth have been homeless at one time or another. They have lived in old cars and down by the river. They know what it means to be abandoned. "I remember living in a truck for a year while my dad tried to get odd jobs in yards," says Wayne. "He would ask the lady he worked for if we could take a shower once a week in her house. Then one day he leaves me with my uncle and I didn't see him again. I keep thinking that I will see him whenever we hand out food to the homeless."

Mission trips include serving in soup kitchens, working in Church outreach programs and helping at food banks. Our purpose becomes encounters with the homeless. Each year, we drive to different places but we try to include Skid Row in Los Angeles as our high point.

The third time we visit, the older youth who had been there prepared the newcomers. Ron instructs them, "Put on your stoic face and don't stare." We arrive early evening in July. Total silence shrouds the car as we see row after row after row of poor people sleeping in blankets or tents.

"Look," cries out Les. "He's shooting up right in the open."

CeeCee points to some children huddled against a wall hugging their backpacks. "They look so hungry and miserable."

Les shouts to be heard. "You know what is different. None of them are Native. I thought that only Natives were homeless."

"I'm not as poor as I thought," says Mark as we see a man with no legs pushing himself along by his hands. "I didn't believe you when you told me about this."

Although we encounter homeless everywhere, our yearly Skid Row trip becomes our iconic symbol for how we define ourselves amidst extreme suffering.

In traveling to San Diego, Kansas, Boulder and Flagstaff, we change our mode to eat with street people rather than handing out food. We take time to get to know the people. We exchange names and make friends rather than give handouts. It puts us in the position where we are with them rather than above them with better possessions. We share rather than give.

On each trip we prepare extra food in an assembly line. We find a table where we can place bread, meat, cheese, mustard, chips, fruit, and juice in a brown paper sack. I see Lisa at the end of the table with a magic marker. I stroll over. She is writing "God Bless You" on each sack as it comes down the line. We no longer take food for granted. Lunch used to be about us. Now it becomes a holy practice of giving.

Bishop Marc Andrus of California suggests, "Give them your name and ask them to pray for you. This bestows dignity on them as they contribute something important to us." So we do. Native people on the street will always pray, usually in their own language. Those of other cultures sometimes pray. But all thank us for asking.

Although the Pacific Ocean and our work in Skid Road become the highlight each summer, we thrive by visiting different congregations.

We serve as acolytes, lay readers, and chalice bearers. Sometimes we preach sermons. In Arizona, we begin attending the Native American Program Group in Phoenix. There our youth encounter two Native elders, the Rev. Dorothy Saucedo, Dine and the Rev. Vivian Winter Chaser, Lakota, deacons in the Episcopal Church. They model dignity and unlimited compassion. To this day, they push and encourage our youth to grow.

These trips build connections between what they experience at home and a promising difference. We change activities often, but keep the same format: first time experiences that include something compassionate, fun and reflective.

Along the way we incorporate Native practices in our meetings. Using their own Native spirituality, the youth bless us and the van with an eagle feather and sage whenever we travel. When appropriate we hold ceremonies for family members who now walk in the Spirit World or celebrate important transitions for the youth. These sacred ceremonies cement our unity as a group. It helps to breathe the sacred through our rites as we cope with the difficult.

By 2013, over 150 young people from five different locations across northern Arizona have participated in our group. We rarely have more than thirty each year. Often we split into smaller groups to strengthen relationships. To fund our travels, we publish reports and pictures on social media and ask for donations. The money always appears, although sometimes it arrives at the very last moment.

Signal encounters on our travels shape us. One small group teaches Vacation Bible School every summer at St. John's Episcopal Church in La Verne, California where they develop strong friendships and mentors. Another group joins the congregation at St. John's Episcopal/Lutheran Church in Williams, Arizona where they participate in Christmas parades and activities. Many youth baptisms take place at the Grand Canyon with this congregation. The youth never get tired of trying to hike down to the bottom of the Canyon. A third group visits several congregations in Colorado. They work on discovering employment contacts and improving job skills.

For a while we run a youth drop-in center called the Hozhoni Youth Center in Holbrook to provide a place for kids to go after school. They can play pool or video games or just hang out with guitars and rock music. Some of the older youth run the center and mentor the younger kids. It becomes a training ground for young Natives to care for each other.

During the last three years before my retirement, the emphasis shifts to job training. The young adults prepare for a job market that pays more than fast food minimum wages.

Fifteen young adults sign up for the training. We contact different congregations to ask for support for a week to train three youth at a time. They agree to provide a place to stay (usually the floor of the Church); arrange for congregational members to teach one life skill for a few hours; and to organize visits to places of employment in their area. We pay a small stipend to each youth and provide a business suit as well as the training.

Each group of three youth attends three different locations for one week each. We travel in the van from Missouri to California. They visit large corporations and small businesses, learning everything from cooking to job interviews. At the end of the three years, twelve of the fifteen have jobs and ten attend junior colleges. All but two move away from Northern Arizona to a location more conducive to a healthy future.

In September of 2013, at seventy-three, I retire as youth missioner and move to Albuquerque. The journey does not end. The remaining youth plan their days to include service to street people and vulnerable children. Many have laptops and connect to the community of Natives through the internet. This allows their continuing mentoring from spiritual Native elders like Bishop Stephen Charleston and Bishop Carol Gallagher. Their journey continues.

AUTHOR'S NOTES

The following stories are true. Sometimes several events have been consolidated into one meeting. Responses to questions often take place over time. For their privacy and protection, we refer to the young people by pseudonyms and have blurred their faces in the photographs.

This book describes how to meet youth where they are. It illustrates encouragement of a minority culture. Each of the following three sections chronicles a journey of self-discovery and healing transformation.

1. *Changing Images to Promote Growth.*

2. *Reclaiming Stories to Restore Dignity.*

3. *Walking a Sacred Path to Give Meaning.*

A profile of a Native youth appears at the end of each section to clarify the journey.

SECTION ONE
Changing Images to Promote Growth

"Show respect to all people, but grovel to none. Always give a word or sign of salute when meeting or passing a friend, or even a stranger, if in a lonely place."
—Tecumseh

Native American Program Group, AZ

Soup Kitchen, Whitter, CA

Changing Images to Promote Growth

"Yeah, my teacher says low esteem remains my main problem." Henry laughs as he mills around with six other teens. They talk over the many times people in authority have told them "what their problem is."

Henry mimics his math teacher. "If you would just apply yourself…"

Les shakes his finger like his probation officer. "Les, you could do so much more if you just pay attention."

Glen plops down in a chair next to me. He wears his baseball hat to flatten his hair. He fights with his teacher every day about removing his hat in class. He loses every day but doesn't give in. The other six kids drift around our small room loaned to us by a church in Winslow.

"So, what's this low esteem about?" asks Glen, carefully looking around the empty table,

Sensing a possible argument, the teens slowly sit down in chairs that are more or less close to the table. Most of the kids sit in the chairs backward or sideways.

I look at the kids with some trepidation. Talking about negative images has erupted into ugly scenes in the past.

"What's the point?" Glen asks.

"People tell me that I will turn out like all the other girls my age, pregnant and ending up with a guy who beats me," says Monica. "I used to believe that before we, you know, started doing new stuff. So how do we get new images?"

For an hour, we talk about images that direct our actions. Some bring pain, like remembering being scared all the time. Some soothe us, like when we recall our grandmother holding us.

We continue discussing images that either paralyze or encourage us for the next twelve years. The youth choose these four basic images to incorporate into their journey

Four Foundational Images:

1. Seeing Goodness in Life

2. Understanding Past as Treasure

3. Knowing the Future as Open

4. Experiencing Self as Valued

Seeing Goodness in Life

Whatever our situation, even in the most horrible and miserable ones, wholeness can appear.

"How can you even suggest that there is something good about this?" asks Buddy who constantly experiences physical abuse at home. He shifts from one foot to another. He called me to come over and stay with him. We stand outside his trailer home listening to the shouting inside.

"I don't mean good as likable." I bite my lip. "I mean good as in wholeness, like seeing a wounded forest flourish again. If we can accept what happens as only a part of the whole, we can let it grow us without turning bitter. We don't have to carve off those pieces of the world that we dislike. Insights come from challenges."

He twists his fingers tighter. "I sort of know what you mean. I hate being fearful all the time. I want to walk in beauty no matter what."

We stand in silence until the voices inside diminish. Buddy straightens his shoulders and thanks me for coming. Slowly he climbs the steps and opens the trailer door. He gives a thumbs up and enters. I drive away.

Understanding Past as Treasure

Whatever has happened in the past, we have a choice about how to relate to it — as a chain holding us back or as a treasure box where we discover more about ourselves.

"I'm so messed up," Marty blurts out when I pick him up from the probation office. "Everyone looks at me like I'm going to do something wrong because I usually do. No one trusts me."

"Your past remains your past," I respond. "It can only stop you if you let it."

"I guess if I move away and get a job somewhere else, no one will know me."

"You will know," I lift one hand from the steering wheel and motion toward him. "You can't run away from yourself. You can learn from some parts and tolerate the others. We all do that to move beyond hurtful things."

Marty lifts his head up and says, "That's what my brother tells me. He moved to Phoenix to escape and just got into trouble there. I don't know how to learn from my mistakes. It just eats me up."

"You know what I'm going to suggest," I say. "Make a list of whatever eats you up. Draw a line beside it and write what you can learn from it. Go from there."

He laughs. "Okay, I'll try it. But I'm coming back if it doesn't work."

"I'll be here." I pick up my keys and grin at him. He jumps in my van and I drive him home.

Knowing the Future as Open

Our future beckons from an open window. We can change. We can choose another way.

Sherry, a sixteen-year old who drinks daily, presses her lips together. "I can't change. I've tried and I just slip back into what I always do. I need a miracle for something new to happen." Five of us in the youth group have gathered in the library's private room in Holbrook, Arizona, for a meeting.

Danny jumps to his feet. "You are the miracle. You have changed totally since I first saw you. You actually care what happens to you. And I've seen you care for homeless people with awesome kindness. You change all the time."

Sherry tears up as the group claps.

Experiencing Self as Valuable

We have a distinctive self.

"You can tell me about my uniqueness all you want. No one cares if I live or die." Ricky curls up on the passenger's side of the van. How do I convince this child that he is cherished when his family reviles him.

I cough a few times to clear my throat. "When have you felt special?" I wait for a long time as he considers this.

He uncurls and straightens out his long legs. "When you took us to the ocean in Los Angeles for the first time, I couldn't believe that you included me and even raised money for me to go. I felt so good inside. I felt like somebody."

We process in silence for the rest of the drive.

I think of the incredulous faces of teens who realize that they have been taken seriously, recognized, or approved in spite of being labeled as mistakes. Every spiritual journey begins with the understanding of being cherished unconditionally.

As the youth group lean toward these perspectives, they begin a healing journey. The next fifteen stories on images illustrate our discussions.

Paths Crossing, AZ

FOUR IMAGES THAT REFLECT GOODNESS IN LIFE

Image 1: Common Dirt Goodness

Even when our lives drip misery goodness can still surprise us.

As I drive down a dark street in Holbrook, Arizona, I see Jake limping down the sidewalk. I stop and offer him a ride. His face tightens as he struggles to climb into the van.

We drive in silence. Since I don't know where to take him, we drive up and down streets.

"Do you want to talk about it?" I ask. He shakes his head but starts talking.

"I was walking home thinking about things. As I got to the cross street, a car full of yelling kids piled out and jumped me. I never even noticed them driving up." He falls silent momentarily.

"Just don't give me any garbage about learning something from this," he fumes, looking out the window. Blood drips from the slash on his face. "There is nothing good about being assaulted by a gang."

He continues with some heat, "I hate those conversations we have in youth group about life being good. It's not for me." He slams his fist into the side window so hard that the van shakes.

We pull into our usual all-night café and find a booth in the back corner. We slowly sip our hot drinks and sit in silence.

Looking out the café's window I see four of our youth group enter the door laughing and jostling each other. They wave at us, then lower their hands as they see Jake's dried blood and bruises. After getting hot drinks, they saunter over to our booth and sit down. No one wants to minimize Jake's experience by offering superficial comments so we sit quietly. Customers walk by our booth and stare at this white haired lady surrounded by Native youth. We lean forward to whisper about the issue, trying not to disturb others.

I talk briefly about the gang. "Jake raises questions of how 'goodness' fits into this."

Danny, one of our older youth at nineteen, pulls his shoulders back and puts his hands on the table. "Things happen that don't feel good. To accept stuff as an opportunity and not as bad or good has to be the hardest lesson I learned. When I turned eighteen, I put in applications at every motel, fast food place, and gas station in town. They all said they weren't hiring. I don't know why but every time I was turned down it just made me work harder. Something happened to me during my search. I felt good about not giving up."

Jake says "Well, nothing good can come out of my being beaten up."

"This has nothing to do with something nice coming from the event." I fold my fingers together as I look around at their serious faces. "Our attitude makes the difference. If we assume that the situation devastates us, it will. If we assume the promise of beauty and goodness, we stay open to possibilities. I don't know how else to say it."

Danny speaks again while lightly punching Jake on the arm. "I used to think like a victim with resentment pouring out of me. That changed one day. Someone in our group said to label the crap I felt as 'given to me' rather than 'done to me.' I had just been kicked out of my home with a black eye. I felt like a fool but I tried it. I walked outside my home and muttered, 'An abusive family has been given to me and I can choose how I go from there.' I felt lightheaded. Using those words jolted me out of being a loser to being in charge. I couldn't believe that words could change me so much."

A respectful silence follows these words. I remember the many times I have immersed myself in victim-like thinking. I'm a little envious that Danny spoke to the heart of the problem.

Arron looks directly at Jake. "You sound like life is out there just waiting for a chance to dump on you rather than lots of chances to try something else. My grandmother told me that our story of walking in beauty doesn't mean lying in the dirt. It means seeing ourselves as welcomed by creation."

Jake manages a crooked smile. "My grandmother used to say something like that too."

We leave the café remembering other times when we saw our lives as ill-fated. "What if goodness is always there, like common dirt?" asks Arron. "I know that I can see the negative and the positive in the same event depending on my attitude. What if we could always choose to see goodness?"

Image 2: Picture of Wholeness

Five of us sit at a table in the church hall in Holbrook, Arizona. A guest tells us "Prayer solves everything. You just have to have the right prayer."

Edwin erupts with a string of curses. "That's bulls##t. Prayer didn't keep my grandmother alive."

He slams his palms against the table. "I prayed for God to not take away my grandmother. She died in pain. What good is prayer? What good is God if he can't help us?"

I don't know what to say. I only know to be there for him. When someone grieves, theological beliefs cannot reach the depth of pain. Being present and acknowledging loss become the most I can do. I want to show tenderness but my grief at his suffering blocks my emotions.

In anguish, he looks repeatedly at me. "I hate you. Leave me alone. Everything you say is s##t. There's no way out. I hate God."

The kids around the table look up at me through half closed eyelids, afraid of their own feelings. Their immobile faces reveal fear at my being challenged. Looking furtively at Edwin, they open their mouths and quickly shut them as though the wrong words might emerge. They sit in the chairs backward or tilted sideways. Chairs cannot contain the energy that spills over from the constant movement of the kids. A Native wood carving rests in the table center. Someone is always picking it up and caressing it with nervous hands. Some of the teens mutter to Edwin, "We're there for you. I've been there. Hold on." The wood carving is passed around from hand to hand like a security blanket.

A week later, Edwin sees me on the street. After a few false starts he asks. "I don't get it. I don't get the 'god' thing. Could we talk about it at group?" I nod and we arrange to meet at Rafe's grandparent's living room.

Sharon begins our meeting with her issues. "I feel like everything is a fake. There is no god, no peace, no love, no future, no nothing. I want to know who God is and what it has to do with me."

Nine teens sitting in every imaginable position on the floor and couch look at me. I feel like hiding. I can't handle this. I start talking hoping something helpful will fall out of my mouth.

"Asking what God 'is' limits us," I say. " It turns God into something that can be defined and restricted to something small. Everyone think of your biggest picture of God. Nod when you have it."

They look at each other. Some squint their eyes or wrinkle their forehead as though making a great mental leap. After a few moments, they nod.

"Okay," I say. "Whatever you came up with as a picture of God, it's too small." Snorting and groans fill the living room. Cries of 'unfair' scatter through the air.

My mouth dries up. "It seems easier saying what *God is not*. God does not appear as Santa Claus, a fix-it God, a supply depot, or a drive through God that gives you what you order. All of these images of God assume a super human who can be manipulated into giving us what we want. It doesn't show you God as the foundation of everything."

Nick raises his hands in mock surrender. "Okay, we know about the '*not*'. " Say something we can get."

"Definitions are out," I say. "We use metaphors and symbols, not labels, to point to something sacred. Think of when a sense of wonder came over you. That's about all I know for sure. For me God is like falling into a moving river where I swim below the surface."

"So, do we pray to a river?" Nick asks.

"No, I get what you mean," says Sharon. "I hate the picture of some white god with a robe—that's just empty space. I feel drawn sometimes to beauty beyond trite words."

I ask, "What are some metaphors that points to something profound and all-encompassing?"

They offer several images: "I think about the ocean waves that polish shells." "For me, it's like the wellspring on the rez that gives fresh water from a hidden spring." "Maybe it's like a pine tree that branches out to shade us."

Rafe settles into his cushion. "How do I know that what I feel has to do with God and not my imagination?"

I straighten my back as something pops into my mind. "Think about this. We get out of the car at the grocery store and see a woman and her kids getting food out of a trash bin. Suddenly compassion moves us. Our own problems don't seem so large. Superficial incidents turn profound. It just happens. The Holy meets us all the time. Staying awake to it makes the difference."

"This goes through my heart like a train zipping by," Edwin says. He dodges a pillow that Sharon throws at him. "I can almost see it and then it disappears. I get that something happens that jolts me, like seeing a kid eat garbage. I respond by giving out good food. I don't always get a feeling that something holy happens. Can you explain this in a few words?"

I pause. "God cannot be contained as an on-call rescue god, waiting above us to swoop in and save us. Wholeness comes when we allow ourselves to see through the ordinary to the Holy. Even the name 'god' with all its old images of being far away can keep us from experiencing the sacred."

Edwin asks, "What do we do though?"

Benny answers. "Fool, we look for times where we feel whole."

Several weeks later, Benny walks toward me with his arm around his girl. "I told her what we said and she doesn't get it. We mean God when something returns us to wholeness and takes us to a deep place, right?"

I say "Too right!" We all laugh and go our separate ways.

With that a journey of growing profoundly begins.

Image 3: Managing Hard Times

The call tone shocks me awake. I fumble for the cellphone.

"Can you come get me? George whispers.

"Where are you?" I ask.

"Home. I have to get out of here."

I throw on my clothes and race toward my van. It's after midnight and the Holbrook streets are mostly empty. I park a half block from his trailer home and walk to the back. George appears and drops his younger brother out the window and then follows. In darkness we hurry back to the van. George keeps touching his bruised cheekbone. His brother holds his arms tight against his chest.

George mutters "Thanks.

I don't know where to take them. I suggest "Want to get a hot chocolate?" Their heads bob up and down.

We reach the drive-through and pick up hot drinks and fries. As we sip the drinks in the van, I ask "Do you want to talk about it?"

The younger brother starts crying.

George struggles to keep a steady voice. "I didn't think he was that drunk and I couldn't get out of the way of his fist. I really got scared when he started swinging at both of us. Can you take us to our Aunt's house on the west side?"

I don't know her so I have some anxiety about dropping off her nephews in the middle of the night.

On the way, George says "I thought that when my stepdad got a job, the fighting would stop. I thought that I could handle everything. I'm just not big enough to stop him."

The aunt accepts them nonchalantly and I drive away.

The next day I pick up Danny at his house and ask if he will talk to the brothers. Danny has helped me before by sharing his experience with the younger kids. He knows the background of these youth and I trust his insights.

"Do you know what you will say?" I ask.

"No," he replies with a sly smile. "Not yet, but it will come to me."

We spot the brothers on the sidewalk after school. Danny hollers, "Get in the van. We need to talk." They grin and climb into the van.

"Listen." Danny laces his hands together. "It is not about growing bigger. Even I am not big enough to fight everyone who is big. We have to grow inside and learn how to make our lives what we want. It starts with accepting your situation as a challenge. We are Native so live in beauty and respect yourself. What happens at home sucks. And it may not get better. But you and your brother can choose to be strong inside. Find the things that make you feel good, like music or sports or hanging out with good friends. You can't change anyone but yourself."

Both brothers seem to take courage from this. George turns to me and says "You can take us home. Everyone will be sober by now." I take them back. The mother stands in the doorway wearing disheveled clothing. One of the windows has a broken pane. The brothers walk past her. No one speaks.

Danny and I wave good-by and drive to a café for coffee. We sit down with our drinks. I keep staring at my coffee cup as though some insights might appear. "Thanks Danny, do you have more words about how they can see the challenge in this drama?"

Danny shakes his head. He draws on the wet spot on the table. "When this happened to me, I remember blaming God, my family, and the lousy hand I kept getting. It took a long time to stop thinking that the dice were against me. We never know what will be offered to us up the road. So we get ourselves ready to face anything and get ready to move on when we can. I know it is hard for the young one but he has to learn that he makes his own future. He can't heal if he can't see something different."

As I think about the wisdom of this nineteen-year old, I realize that I am still learning to choose my response to whatever happens. I don't know what my last decades will bring, but I know that I too can prepare by being strong inside.

Image 4: Generous Outlook

Edwin stumbles into the living room yawning. Rolland calls out, "Hey Dog, didn't you get any sleep last night."

"No, we had too much drama. I woke up at 2 a.m. thinking 'It's all a hoax. God doesn't exist.'"

Since we don't have a regular meeting room, someone's grandparents let us use their living room. Four teens sit on the floor. Five others drape themselves over the worn couch.

"Is this wrong?" asks a young girl with her three-month baby on her lap. Others chime in: "Am I going to hell for …" "Is it wrong to follow the red road?" "Why do I have to choose between my tradition and the Jesus way?" "What makes something a sin?" "Why do missionaries tell us we have to believe their way?" "Do we have to believe in some blonde haired, blue eyed god to stop being poor?" "Why are Christians so mean and sad all the time?"

"What do you believe?" I ask Sophie who shifts her baby to her other arm.

"I believe what my grandmother tells me. She says it is important to respect all living things. And to share what I have," Edwin says.

I remember the times when they dug into their pockets for change to give to a homeless person. "Do you share with everyone or just with Natives?" I ask.

Wide eyes and open mouths look up at me. "You are kidding, right?" says Edwin. "Mother Earth and Father Sky cover everyone. Creation is open to all."

Rolland jumps in. "My grandmother taught me to look at everything as sacred including people we don't like or stuff like trees."

"Why don't you tell us what you believe in?" demands Sophie.

With unmoving eyes, they fix on my face. "I believe that generosity keeps us connected to wholeness. Our spiritual path keeps us looking for the wonder in front of us and responding in open-hearted joy to those we encounter. The dignity we show when we give away our coat or let someone sleep in our house wells forth from our being generous. Jesus walked this way. So did your ancestors."

Nick holds up one of our cameras. "I think our photographs say a lot about how we are generous. Look at how many pics we have of us laughing or talking with those on the street or the sunrise or other awesome things. We remember the full times."

Rolland rubs the back of his neck, "I look at people and know when they are superficial or mean. I don't agree with a lot of what people think I should believe. I believe I am connected to God in a binding way that pulls me to be compassionate and think deep. I'm not sure about Jesus but I think he had a generous soul. Maybe I see God through Jesus. I'm not certain."

Edwin, who has recently been released from Juvie says, "When the others saw me praying in my cell, they called me god-boy. I told them that I rather be a god-boy than a f**k-up. My grandmother lets strangers into our house to eat. She shares whatever she has. That remains my tradition."

We continue to exchange stories about generosity. They never run out of questions about the richness of their traditions.

FOUR IMAGES THAT REFLECT PAST AS TREASURE

Image 5: Tradition as Guide

We sit under a large tree in the park throwing pine cones at each other. When we stop playing, I start the meeting. "When we created the Spirit Journey Youth, we wrote rules. The first one you chose reads 'Honor Sacred Ground.' Tell me about that."

No one speaks. I wait it out. More pine cones are thrown.

Finally, Rafe ventures a comment. "If God is there, it's holy."

Edwin snorts. "That makes everything holy then."

We laugh and I wait again. The leaves on our tree tremble with the breeze. It seems a long wait.

"When we pay attention to what we really see and don't let our posturing get in the way, we notice deep things, like the importance of family." Rafe seems intent on digging up the grass in front of him as he talks.

Danny speaks up, "I think it happens in two ways. When we mark it with sage or corn pollen, like when we celebrate something or remember someone walking in the spirit world. It also happens when something good happens, like when we shared our food with those on skid road in L.A. and we all felt something hard core."

"I know what you mean." Rafe continues to dig up the grass in front of him. "For me, it is when we stop and really notice someone hurting, or thank the animals before we eat hamburgers. It's stopping and noticing. Usually that happens when we see something unexpected like the seals in the ocean or when we look deeply inside for strength so we don't go ballistic."

"Sometimes when we talk about good things that happen, it happens again. Our energy multiplies just by reminding ourselves of awesome stuff," says Sherry. "The spirit is in everything, so when we look at an awesome petrified log we can actually connect."

"Do other races have sacred ground? asks Rafe. "One of my school friends took me to his church service and got mad when I talked during the prayer. He said that the church building was holy. I told him it was not holier than our four sacred mountains. We argued so loud that others started shushing us."

We chuckled at that story. Others begin talking about misunderstandings that happen if they talk with non-natives about their sacred practices of burning sage, or spreading pollen in the four directions or running toward the sun in the morning."

"I don't think God means the same to other people as it does to us," says Edwin. "Kids I know don't ever talk about what is holy."

Danny says, "Maybe they don't know. Maybe it's up to us to show them."

My mind swirls with these discussions. From the beginning of our journey together, the youth talk so casually about their experience of the holiness of creation. My heart aches that these children have been so cruelly labeled as superstitious yet understand deeply their connection to the sacred.

Image 6: Being Complete

Driving to a teen's house, I see his youngest sibling playing by an old car. The father comes out and yells at her. She cowers, dodges a blow and creeps sideways into the house. My heart constricts thinking about the loud voices and potential violence she endures. "Can I go inside your house to speak to your son?" I ask.

He grunts and points toward the door. I enter to find Drew hugging his sister on the couch. We talk briefly and I leave.

Later in the week as I am driving in Winslow, AZ, Arron waves me over. "Can we have a meeting? Some of the younger guys have encountered some rough stuff at the school."

"Sure," I say. He gets in the van and we drive around to pick up four of the Junior High students. We drive to the Winslow Church and settle in the youth room at the back.

I sit on a chair as they collapse onto floor cushions. "Tell me about it."

Drew lifts up his head. "I hate that everyone knows everything about my family, especially the arrests. I'm so tired of my teachers telling me that I shouldn't be like my older brothers. They have no right to judge me by my family's past."

"How do you judge yourself?" I ask.

"How did you know?" he laughs. "Sometimes I think I will never get rid of the bad parts of my past. I just wish there were more good parts." He pulls his cap low on his forehead and falls silent.

"I hate it when tourists stare at me and clutch their purses like I am a thief because I'm Native." Rolland flinches as though he sees the tourist in front of him. He shakes his head. "I did steal when I was younger but I am trying to be different. Sometimes at night I just run really fast. It's not that I have somewhere to go; I run to get away from me."

"Yeah," says Sammy. "Every time I think I am free from past stuff, like getting drunk and smashing windows, I just know that I'm going to fall into that trap again. I'm never going to get rid of my past."

I pause. "None of us can get rid of our past. We can integrate it but we can't be rid of it. For me, the past screams for me to accept it as a whole."

Sammy nods at this. "I know that I am not very old but my values keep changing. Things I hated or mistrusted have changed into things that I have learned from. When my dad used to nag me about being responsible, I thought he was full of it. Now, I get it. I'm going to nag my children the same way. I don't want them arrested because they didn't think."

Arron stretches his neck as he looks around the room. "A couple of years ago, my uncle told me that I was going to be like my dad, a useless cokehead. I yelled at him and came close to hitting him. I ran out of the house, bitter about everything." Arron looked around the room and met the stares of each kid. "We met as a youth group and talked about how to integrate the good and the bad parts of our history. We scribbled down our major past events and the approximate dates. We wrote down what we had learned or how we had been changed by each event. Then we were asked to choose which event we would shed. As we talked about how we had learned from even the worst stuff, I began to see that my past has shaped me. I like who I am now. In some way, it completes me. Maybe I am only whole if I include everything that has happened."

Lee draws his knees up to his chin and clears his throat. We turn to look at him. "I visited my friend and saw a man who looked so much like my uncle, who raised me in love and generosity. Then he spoke. It turned out to be my dad who had left us twelve years ago. Perhaps if I had known he was there and not seen him as the face of my uncle, I would have beat him up for all the things he did to me and my mother.

But I saw a Native like the uncle I loved and I saw myself. I felt all mixed up. Evil and good fought in my stomach. Instead of hitting him I found myself shaking his hand and saying to myself, 'It's okay.' Finally, I put to rest my hatred. Maybe it was one of those god-events we talk about."

"What do you mean?" demands Sharon, playing with her braids.

He turns to face her. "When something bad turns good, or something we thought was hopeless turns out to be hopeful, we call it 'one of those god-things.' It means that we look at something differently. I like the image Arron gave us of wholeness. It makes me think I can move on beyond the bad stuff."

Looking around, I could see the healing take place in their breathing. Accepting their past as an integral part of them fills up a hole that held bitterness. This begins the frame for future discussions on completeness.

Image 7: Practicing Connections

"Nothing on the rez helps me fit into getting a job or live in a large city." George stares at his palms as he talks. "I saw on the History Channel where a bunch of white people traveled to Tibet searching for God. What's that about?"

I make myself comfortable on my chair in the community hall. "When people don't fit in, they go looking for their destiny somewhere else. Our traditions tell us something different."

George tilts forward in his chair. "Which tradition—our Rez one, the youth group, family, this church, which?

These nine teens straddle between two cultures that do not balance well. I hate being pinned down to saying definitively what someone's tradition states when I do not have clarity. But when they hunger for some understanding of how their customs make sense, I attempt to explain. "In your indigenous tradition, something powerful connects with us first. We do not have to seek anyone or anything. Mother Earth and Father Sky cover us all." I pause trying to gather my thoughts. "We only have to be open to deepening those times when the profound happens."

Drew almost falls off his chair as he leans toward me. "I don't get it. What are we open to?"

I start rubbing my shoulder to gain time. "We don't have to climb mountains to find deep experiences. Wondrous things happen to us all the time. Like when we walk in skid road in L.A. and we see great personalities beyond the everyday label of 'homeless.' Or when we hand out food at the soup kitchen to four hundred street people and realize that we enjoy talking to people when we thought it would be a bore. Being open cuts across different ethnic traditions. How many of you have been taught to share and respect even strangers or to give thanks for all things in Creation?"

Many nod at this last question. Then Sophie waves her hand at me and says, "Yeah, but some people are always bugging me about the one and only way, and the one truth."

Danny says "We are more into connections than into who is right. I was taught to be aware of what is around me rather than trying to find something special. Even on my spiritual quest, I was only told to be awake to anything that came my way. Is that what you mean?"

"Exactly!" I say.

As the teens talk among themselves, I reflect on how much easier it has been to work with Natives who already participate in daily ceremonies that honor the Creator. The first time I saw an Elder sprinkle the corn pollen on the ground and murmur prayers of thanksgiving, I couldn't believe how casual it all seemed. I ask, "What are your earliest memories of the Great Spirit?"

Rafe stands up to look at each person. "Every morning my grandfather sprinkles the corn pollen to the East and thanks the Creator for creating us and giving us this day. As soon as I became old enough I joined him. It fills my heart to be able to greet each day with that connection. The days I don't feel like it, everything turns sour."

Sammy joins in: "I remember my grandmother's stories. They told about how our Creator acts in practical ways to bolster us as noble people and wants us to follow the old ways. I felt uncomfortable when we went to a Christian Church. I don't like being asked to follow another god who judges me and wants me to walk another way. I guess I lost my interest in any kind of religion until I joined the youth group."

George paces up and down in his excitement. "I guess I put my conflict about god away while I just messed up my life. When we discussed this in the youth group I began to think about important influences. I remember how important it felt to me as a child to be Native and do the ceremonies and greet the sun. I don't know how I forgot it. Stuff I used to label as old fashioned now have value."

Drew says. "When we started writing prayers, I wrote them by rote at first. Then we wrote psalms where we had to say how the holy appears. I started remembering things. When we ate with the homeless, I felt in my gut that something we call God or Great Spirit or Creator fills us with happiness and compassion at the same time. It's not like some person gives me happiness. I just feel bigger and more connected to other people, even those I just met on the street. We keep marking holy places and holy times until it seems we marked most of Los Angeles. I'll never forget that. Things fall into place as we stamp the ground holy and sprinkle a little pollen. The God of my ancestors and the God of the Christians seem the same. I belong here. It remains a little mixed up but I have no doubt that something connects with me even when I am stubborn and closed minded."

"The more we practice the old ways, even on the streets of Los Angeles, the more I connect to my ancestors," says Danny. "I feel like my past really does teach me to live in beauty today. The sacred leaks through the past to right now."

We close off our meeting and file out of the library, strangely content in our memories.

Image 8: Merging the Old/New

Chuck joins us under the tree at a turnoff at the Grand Canyon. "Someone just told me that I'm lucky to live off the Rez and not be subject to all that superstition. Even though I am not traditional, that makes me so angry that I want to punch him." He punches the air as the other five youth laugh.

"Every time I hear someone comparing our tradition and saying how superior Christianity is, I want to puke." Edwin mimics vomiting on the ground.

Danny pulls some sage off of a bush and starts rubbing it on his arms and legs.

"What are you doing?" Chuck asks.

Danny replies. "We are at the Grand Canyon. It's sacred to a lot of our people. We traditionally rub native sage on us to let our ancestors know we belong."

Quickly we all find a sage bush and pat ourselves down. We sit in a circle with our backs to trees and breathe slowly.

"I forgot," Edwin says. "I didn't mean to bring negative thoughts here. I just don't know how to be both someone who loves to hear heavy rock music and honor our customs. It gets mixed up in who I am and how different I want to be."

"Fortunately," I say, "we can combine past and present images of ourselves. We don't have to get rid of the past."

Chuck shifts to be closer to the tree. "How do we do that?"

"Everyone scatter and find something in the woods that stands as a metaphor of your past. When you find it, hold it in your hand and say 'this is like (name a value).' Think of something that empowers you and makes you proud."

To my surprise, they immediately go in all directions. They bring back pine cones, rocks, feathers, juniper needles and tree branches. They all talk at once, holding up their object.

Jake begins. "My grandfather taught me how to chop wood when I was really little. He would give me some twigs and hold my hand over the hatchet. He was so patient. When I got tired, he told me that Chees' never quit. So these twigs remind me not to quit." He strokes the twig and puts it in his pocket.

Chuck clutches a rock. "When my family built a barn on the rez, we kids had to haul the rocks to build the foundation. It took us several days. I remember asking how long it would take and how many more rocks we had to move. My mother's brother told me 'Don't let a few rocks stop you. There will always be rocks.' That made it better. It made it easier."

Each youth talked about his or her object with a serious tone. It was almost enough.

"One more thing we have to do to let your past inform you about your present image." I stand up to demonstrate. "Everyone stand and take a physical position of strength and pride. Where do you put your feet? Your hands. Your eyes. Do you sway or stand still? As you see, I stand still with my feet planted in the dirt and one hand stretched out with my palm up. Show me how you stand."

After a few false starts and some giggles, everyone takes a stance.

"Pretend you have been frozen into a position of inward strength, like you are facing a fear, or proposing marriage, or something scary." At that they all laugh. "Add the value you named from your past. Change your feet, hands or head to reflect this."

This took about five minutes for the youth to imagine how they would look. To my surprise, they stood taller and raised their heads a bit. I ask, "Do you feel any different?"

Danny looks around at the group. "I thought this exercise would be too silly to do but I find myself glad. I like remembering the good things of our customs. Somehow I feel taller."

THREE IMAGES THAT REFLECT FUTURE AS OPEN

Image 9: Finding Alternatives

"I don't want to graduate," confides Nick, a high school senior. "There will be a big party with all my relatives and people will be happy that I walked. But then it's over. Nothing goes on after that." He slumps down in his chair.

Six more youth drive into the parking lot of the cafe, see my car, and come to find us at our usual booth.

"How do the rest of you think about this?" I clean my glasses to avoid pressure by looking directly at them.

"I used to think the same," says Arron who straightens up in his chair. "Most of my friends do nothing after high school. Sure they try to get jobs but classes gave them something to look forward to every day even though they hated school. And to get into college takes effort and money. Even to move away takes effort. No one does it for you."

Sammy clears his throat. "I've spent my time running away and taking care of myself. It seems tough not being in school and having someone else telling you what to do. But I had some experience of making decisions on my own. A counselor bugged me to figure out what I want to do. That turned me around. I had a vague picture of wanting something else but not until I decided to finish my GED did I actually do something. Then other goals started to become more defined. But I had to take the first step on my own. I won't lie. I have never done a more difficult thing."

Nick swallows hard, "I don't think I can do that. It all seems a dead end. I don't have anything in me that even wants to make a goal. I don't want anything that bad."

Sherry shakes her long brown hair. "I used to be like that. My head was totally into this town. I would see losers on the street and think how I would be like that in twenty years. When we visited different cities, I saw how many different things there are out there that I can do. Part of me believed that new things were out there and part of me didn't think I could do anything different."

"I think I'm finally getting that," says Nick. "Each time we go somewhere and people ask me what I want to do, I begin to believe that maybe I can do something different."

We continue talking as more of the kids open up to their anxieties of choosing options. On each trip away from their small town, they meet people who assume that these young Natives can dream full-size and accomplish greatly. Once in Colorado, our host took us to an assisted living home where the youth played bingo with the seniors. I sat in the back of the room and watched with pleasure as they listened to life stories from the elders. On our ride home, they told me about the suggestions and questions that residents gave to them. Nick pushes his baseball cap back on his head. "They were really interested in what I wanted to do with my life. One old man listed twelve different jobs he tried before he became a mechanic. I didn't realize how many types of jobs existed. Whoever heard of hiring someone to select songs on a radio station?"

Accepting that they have a do-able future releases them to change even when their fears seem so large.

Image 10: Starting Over

"Well, I messed up big time." Chuck talks to me across a table in the County Juvenile Detention facility. He bangs his head against the table. The guard looks over at us frowning. "My grandfather and everyone else in my family tell me how much I disappoint them. You say that we can start again but I don't buy it. There are just so many chances you get in life and I have used them all up."

I hold my hands up in mock surrender. "Are you buying in to someone else's judgment? Where do these evaluations come from? Who says you messed up? Have you been judging yourself? Or what?"

"I'm in jail, what do you think?" A sneer covers his face.

"I think you are in pain and my flip answer didn't help." My voice fades out as I apologize.

"No," shaking his head. "You are right. I down myself too much and I shouldn't be listening to how people try to chop me down."

"Which of your actions came out of boredom and which out of malice or anger?" I ask.

He lifts his head slightly. "Drinking came out of boredom and slashing tires came out of malice."

"So, in terms of criminal activity, you didn't use force or a gun or rape or anything that caused serious damage except for the tires. If you were the judge, what would you say about you?"

He grins "I would say that I am a no good kid who only gets into trouble."

"And if God sat in the judgment seat, what might the Creator say?" I hold my breath, dreading his answer.

"I give up." he shrugs.

"Humor me," I insist. "Tell me about three times you had a new chance to start over again."

After several minutes of thinking he starts, "The first time I was arrested, I got probation and not jail time; when I told my girlfriend I was sorry she took me back; and when I mouthed off at one of the adults at the church, he talked to me about it and we became friends. He even welcomed me back the next year."

"And did you deserve another chance in any of these situations?"

"No." He curls his lip. "You are trying to tell me something, aren't you?"

"Yes. What do you think?" I sit back in my chair waiting and hoping.

He offers several incomplete sentences. Then he stops and takes a deep breath. "That I get a new chance even if I don't want it or deserve it."

"You got it," I grin.

He grins back.

We say goodbye and I sit in my van thinking about this conversation. Each time I see one of the youth accompanied by a guard, I want to quit in frustration. Then Chuck inspects a new possibility; that he can start over again even when he doesn't deserve it.

With that image of mercy, we plunge back into our healing journey.

Image 11: Beyond Ashes

"I don't get it." Rolland slouches in his chair. "Why make such a big deal out of Easter? You don't believe that stuff, do you?"

I turn still as I go inside my memories to reach for something deep and practical. Eleven members of the youth group have dye on their hands, clothes and everything in sight. Sitting in the Winslow church hall we have fun making outlandish Easter eggs for the homeless. They look up at me at Rolland's question.

"What do you think about Easter?" I ask

Jake shrugs and says, "It doesn't make sense to me—something about a cross and empty tomb. I saw a cartoon on it once. It seemed silly."

"You have the basic story elements—death and life." As I approach my seventh decade, more people die that I have known a long time. It hurts when death takes away someone I love and ends a good life. I understand intellectually that everything and everyone dies. But when it happens, I hurt. The Easter story talks about death in a new way. In the Christian tradition, Easter counts as the defining moment of the early Church. Parts of the story seem totally unbelievable. But it sets the pattern of dying to old stuff before we can live as new. It's core."

"What have been some of the defining moments in your life?" I settle in my seat.

Drew pushes his baseball cap back on his head. "Something happened to me when we took a homeless man to lunch in skid row. I had never eaten with someone living on the street. At first it scared me, but then I realized that I had been foolish. These people walk and talk just like me. We went up to a man with a hoodie and told him that we had a little extra money and would he like to go eat with us. He looked at my dark skin and smiled."

"Sure, thanks," he said. The three of us went to a sandwich shop and got a burger, fries and a coke. We sat down at a booth. I noticed that other people stared at him as though he doesn't belong. We started talking. It didn't take long before my distrust of the man melted. He talked about sports teams and where he had lived and what he hoped for. I was angry that I had spent so much time being distrustful and even fearful. After that I see their faces, not just the backpacks and dirt."

I turn to the others. "What other events define your life beside skid road?"

"For me," Danny replies, "it happened when we returned to Arizona from a mission trip. I met a dude I didn't like. We used to fight all the time. Then we saw a dog being run over and killed in Hopi Street. We looked at each other and I didn't want to fight anymore. After that I changed. I didn't want to go back to old habits. I smiled and talked to people on the street. I used to ignore everyone. Even my step dad said that I had changed. I don't know what I was so scared of before. Since then I feel like things will open up for me. So far it has. I moved to a new state, I got an apartment; I'm going to community college. It's all good."

"If you could say what Easter means in a few words, what would you say?" I ask.

"I have a story," cries out Rafe shoving his hands in his pockets. "On the Rez, we had a tree in front of our Hogan. We used to play all the time in that old tree. Once after a storm, it died. We were stunned. It was our only tree. Eventually the tree fell over. We started playing on top of it, jumping on and off. It became our favorite place to play even though it was dead and in pieces. So I guess Easter is about something dying and you find something new anyway."

Nick says "Yeah, that's good," drawling out his words. "The tomb stood empty, and good stuff still happened after that."

We finish dying the eggs and clean up the room. As everyone leaves, Danny turns to me to say, "When my younger sister died, her death made me think beyond the immediate problems I was having in school. I hated her dying but I had to become a different brother to my younger siblings. I started doing things for them that I had never done. That has something to do with Easter."

As I lock up, I think about the Easter promise and how it relates to these Native youth. In everyday minutiae, the Natives walk a spiritual path of dying and discovering new paths. They face the fear of things not lasting, of death meaning an end of something good, and a drastic change that is a challenge to once familiar issues. Traditional Christian belief remains fuzzy, but they know the story of something big emerging from the ashes.

FOUR IMAGES THAT REFLECT SELF AS VALUED

Image 12: Being Good Enough

Zach slings his cap on the kitchen table. "I want to get out of this town." Six of the youth group and I have been invited to Zach's grandparents' house for a meeting.

We discuss the possibility of moving to a larger city. Our small town has been slowly dying. Relatives and friends keep moving to cities that have more employment possibilities.

George confesses, "I don't think I am ready yet. I need to build up some good things in myself before I can make it in another place." He shifts around on his chair.

Zach fiddles with the pencils on the table. All the kids squirm unless they can touch or chew something. "What do you mean?" he asks.

"I'm not strong enough to change. I need to wait until I know I can make it." George chews the pencil in his mouth.

"You may wait forever." Arron throws an empty cup at him as he says this. "You think you will ever be good enough?" I remember when I didn't say anything in the group because I thought I didn't have anything to say. I was going to wait until I got smart enough. But then we went around the table and I said something. No one told me it was stupid. I got into the habit of saying what I thought and then I realized that the more I spoke the better I got at what I was saying. If I had waited until I was good enough, I never would have been good enough. Just saying…"

I carefully line up my pencils and pens. "Tell me about the things we did before we knew we could."

"Remember when we first went to the ocean?" George says. "I said that nothing will ever get me to swim with sharks. I was so scared. I found myself running into the sea with my clothes on without thinking. I was dripping and even ruined my shoes. That became the best thing I have ever done. I can't imagine who I would be today without my swimming in the Pacific." George picks up his big feet and shows us his new shoes.

"I remember when you first told me that I will carry in the candle during the service. You turned away before I could tell you I didn't know how. Then the deacon arrives and says 'Here's the candle.'" I thought if everyone believes I can do it, then I can do it." Zach's voice shakes a little.

"We still do a lot of stuff like that." Edwin's face lights up. "We walk up to someone's rich home and you tell us, 'Eat whatever they serve you, say thank you, and talk during the conversation.' We just walk on in. I am doing things I never thought I could do in a house where the swimming pool is larger than my house."

We start laughing as we remember all the new things we have tried and how different we have become.

"They never knew we had been in jail or on drugs or nothing. We did so many new things that my family did not believe me when I got back. We still do new things." Chuck gives a mock salute to the group.

"Yeah, my friends think I am bragging because I do more in a summer than they have done in their lives," Edwin says. "When I tell my little brother, he thinks I make it up but he listens."

After our meeting we thank the grandparents and wave goodbye to each other. It feels as though we have completed only the first layer of being "good enough." Later in the year, I hear the youth talking about waiting for the day when they "grow up" or hoping that change will happen when they prove themselves by getting a girlfriend or a good job. I smile to myself when I finally hear one of the guys saying "Ready or not, I'm going for it."

The self-discovery of being "good enough" takes time.

Image 13: Cleaning the Slate

One summer day I sit with the youth at the park in Flagstaff. I use a pack of cards containing questions as an ice breaker. I read the first card. "What did you think would send you to hell when you were a child?"

Lisa tentatively raises her hand. "My mother told me that I will go to hell if I lie."

Rafe sprawls on the grass and drawls. "So, what happened?"

"Oh, I lie all the time." She throws her long black hair back. "I figure that I am going to hell anyway."

With that, the others start listing all the things that condemn them. They don't come from a traditional Church background so I don't know where these images of hell originate.

As we talk, I discover that heaven or the eternal has no meaning for them. But they all know about hell.

Rafe straightens up, "My mother got angry once and told me, 'You so bad not even hell will accept you.'" As he says those words, a coil of anger and sadness twist in my stomach. I wish I had never asked this question.

"Hell" remains a lively topic of conversation that takes place over many months within the group.

Once when we travel to Phoenix in our van, the kids start talking. Their voices overlap. "Will I go to hell if I…" "Will I go to hell if I hit my mom?" "Will I go to hell if I have sex in the church?" "Will I go to hell if I hurt someone bad?" "Will I go to hell if I become a drunk?" The questions continue endlessly, not on how to live a godly life but the kind of punishment to expect for being bad to the core.

My mind clouds up as I struggle with the metaphors of heaven and hell. I stop the van at a rest stop so we can talk at a park bench.

I shake my head back and forth. "You can't go to hell."

"You can't know that," Julie snaps back.

"Yes, I do.". "You have goodness inside you and you connect to awesome things, like the snow on San Francisco Peaks or when we laugh at something goofy."

Tears appear in her eyes. I sit there stunned that my response speaks to something deep within her. I look around and see the others looking down, some with red eyes.

I worry about their focus on hell/heaven metaphors that assumes a world of clear cut judgments. Yet "hell" invades their thinking moments. Being on a route to someplace good does not exist for them.

"Let's talk about this," I suggest. I place my yellow legal pad on the table for a reframing exercise. "Let's list all the things you do that merits hell." Answers include drugs, stealing from family, slashed tires, bullying, and uncontrollable violence and lying.

"Now we rename them on a continuum from accidental to hard core bad." The teens have fun with this exercise. "That's poor judgment." "That seems to be ignorance of consequences." "That smells of drunken reactions."

Chuck stands up. "I think we should replace "hard core bad" with "evil."

"No," I say immediately. "Evil comes from another century. It has a superstitious smell to it. It contradicts our inherent goodness as children of the Creator."

"But we did something wrong," Chuck says.

"Of course," I say. "That's why we have unlimited chances to stop doing these things and making things right."

Chuck shrugs. "You aren't like us. Evil is just in us."

"What about your Native ceremonies?" I ask, rubbing my forehead in desperation.

We explore the different traditional ceremonies available (especially for those who had been in war or in violent circumstances). They admit that these Native ceremonies remove the stain so they start over again as those re-centered in beauty.

I tell them Bible stories of prostitutes and thieves being forgiven. Unfazed, sixteen black eyes stare at me.

I get up and walk around. "Does anyone have a story about being judged okay even when he or she has messed up?"

Nick straightens up on the bench to tell this story. "We went to the same church several times on a mission trip. One year I was caught smoking weed in the church and really got told off about my disrespect and my inability to focus because I was so mellowed out. The next year I was asked to go on the mission trip again. That totally knocked me down. I didn't deserve it. When we arrived at the church people treated me like I was their lost son. Everyone, even those who knew what I did the year before, greeted me with such happiness. That's when I decided that maybe I wasn't a lost cause, that I really can have a clean slate."

Jerry puts a grass stem in his mouth and raises his head. "Once I smarted off at my stepfather and he knocked me against the wall. He and his buddies had been drinking and started hitting everyone. My little brother got hit. My mother screams 'Look at what you started.' When my stepfather starts in on my brother, I grab him and hide behind the sofa. I just held on to my brother and told him it was okay. I keep patting him on the back and telling him it was okay. Eventually, the drunks left the house and we came from behind the sofa. I felt so bad about starting this. I know my stepdad has a violent temper."

My aunt starts cleaning up the living room. She stoops down to talk to me. 'Jerry, you know better than to mouth off like that. But you made up for it by protecting your brother. All we can do when we mess up is to make up for it the best we can' She smiles at me as she takes my sobbing brother into the kitchen. I felt like I had been nudged back in the wolf pack and told to learn my lesson." He falls silent, not looking at anyone.

With that, we gathered up our stuff to get back into the van. Chuck puts an arm around Jerry's shoulder and walks him to the van.

Julie asks, "Can we talk about this some more? Not today but at a different meeting." I nod yes.

We continue this discussion for several years. Gradually, I see their negative self- images change as they experience being cherished in spite of their mistakes. As different people welcome them unconditionally into their homes and churches, hell as a backdrop slowly diminishes.

Image 14: In Spite Of

Seven of our older youth take additional training to become the leadership team of the Spirit Journey Youth They hold discussions with our Junior and Senior High kids. For a week the team has been adding and discarding questions for a lesson they will teach on their own.

"Remember, you can't give answers, only hints. They can't learn if you tell them," I caution, managing not to wring my hands.

The day to teach the lesson arrives. We have a mixed group of sixteen teens and young adults. Arron beams at the youth. "Who remembers our favorite story of the employer giving unfair wages?"

No one does so Danny summarizes the story. "There was this dude who was hiring men. He offers to pay something like $100 to get a job done in his yard. So a lot of men start work at 8 am and work all day. At 4 pm in the afternoon, a couple of dudes work for one hour only. The employer pays them all $100, even the ones who only work an hour. How was that fair?"

The kids look at each other and begin to protest. "Totally unfair." "It is totally messed up." "What kind of lesson is that?"

Grinning, the leadership team gives hints, "This is Jesus talking and he is trying to teach us something."

That just gets grunts from the youth. Hank says, "He is not referring to money. What is he talking about?" The kids talk among themselves to figure out what would be fair.

Danny gives a fake moan. "It's not about fair." More guesses are made. The younger kids look at each other with sideward glances.

Finally, Hank shouts, "It's not about deserving the money."

"Oh, I got it." shouts Pete. "It's about that grace thing that we get in spite of what we do." Relief erupts around the table as Arron nods. "So, tell us what this story means."

The young ones work it out. Julie says, "Let's say that you have been helping the street people and going to church and being generous to people your whole life and you feel good about it. Then someone who messes up hard core finally gets it, even if he has not been a good person all his life. He gets to start over the same as the lifetime good guy and is just as loved even though he has wasted most of his life."

"That's it!" cries the leadership team almost in unison. "So what does that mean how you treat people?"

Jake answers, "S**t, that means that we can't look down on street people when we give them food or clothes because they get the same chance we get even if we do feel superior because we are not homeless."

Rafe quips, "Grace is an equal opportunity law."

An air of camaraderie permeates the room as the lesson ends.

Image 15: Shepherds' Example

Christmas time triggers continual headaches for our kids. Mixed messages of greed and superstition abound in our society during this season. The happy family cheerfully preparing for a reunion around a colorful tree remains elusive. The youth absorb images of Santa with copious gifts which they don't usually get.

On the first day of Advent, we sit in a community hall and talk about the relevance of the Christmas message. It meets with mixed reviews.

"I hate Christmas," says Jake. "Everyone gets drunk. They promise me something nice but it never happens."

Lisa says "I keep hoping that Christmas will mean something but it ends up the worst time of the year."

My face freezes. I do not know how to explain a celebration I love. The constant promotion of a fantasy wonderland that revolves around presents blocks my imagination. I schedule another meeting for the next Tuesday after school.

I meet with the leadership group to discuss giving the younger kids alternative images of the holiday.

Danny looks around at the seven of us sitting around a table in the community hall. "Can you tell us what you believe? I have a hard time with Christmas myself."

They fiddle with the glittery stars and trumpets on the table as I gather my thoughts. I find myself turning over and over a small donkey from the nativity set. "I'm not concerned with the details that people argue about. It's the story. An ordinary family with a husband who works with his hands has been asked to be open to something wondrous. A child with power to transform life goes on loan to them. Everything in the story shouts sensation. Angels appear and shepherds run to greet the amazing. Wise people arrive with gifts for a baby found in an ordinary, everyday animal shelter. Could anything better illustrate finding the profound in things you see daily?"

The youth leaders start talking. "How can we come up with something new to get the kids to understand this?" They read the Bible story and choose the part about the shepherds. They argue about insightful questions. Finally, they settle on a plan and Hank agrees to lead the discussion.

The day comes and a group of fifteen kids sit on the floor in a circle. Hank takes a deep breath and reads the story from the Gospel of Luke. "Okay, this story talks about God coming to walk with us rather than being better than us. When the shepherds came to see Jesus and bow down, what do you think about the requirements for entering the manger?"

The kids throw out suggestions. "They had to believe this was the Christ." "They must have come with good hearts, with no bitterness." "They had to be 'good' people, not ghetto rats." "The angels sponsored them."

"Wrong!" Hank answers. "I'll read the story again."

He reads and asks the same question again.

Jake half raises his hand. "It doesn't say anything about them except that they do what the angels told them to do. It doesn't say that they were good or bad. They were just there."

Sammy speaks up, "The angels came to them and told them what was up. They went to check it out. It doesn't say anything about what kind of shepherds they were. It doesn't even say they were good with their sheep."

"So!" The mentor grins widely, "What do you think of the requirements for you to see the Holy?"

Lisa tilts her head. "This is a loaded question, isn't it?"

"Yes," he responds gleefully.

Jake takes a deep breath. "It means the Holy comes to us and doesn't ask how messed up we are. That's why we find ourselves on holy ground when we are talking with the homeless. God doesn't ask us if we are good and doesn't judge the homeless people either."

"That's hard core." Sammy places his hand over his heart. "You would think God would have some requirements of us, like trying to be good, before we could see something as important as the Christ, even if he was just a little baby."

"It's a good thing for us that he doesn't," says Jake pretending to punch Sammy in the arm.

Hank nods his head. "This story shows us about finding the Holy in simple and profound ways."

Energy explodes as we wish each other "Merry Christmas."

NATALIE: Personal story of recovering a self-image of strength.

My daughter says to me: "Why do they stare so hard at us when we come to this store? It scares me. Have I done something wrong?" She looks up at me with her big brown eyes and oval face. Her Native beauty overpowers me.

"No." I bend down to her level. "Some people don't like our skin but we walk proud. We live by our heritage, not by what others think."

My daughter takes my hand. She doesn't realize how long it has taken me to be able to say that.

My mother told me "A woman has a hard life. Find someone to take care of you." But my grandmother would say: "Stay strong, root yourself in the earth and fly with eagles in the sky." I grew up confused by seeing some women who spoke out strong in our Chapter meetings and other women with bruises on their faces who hid in the corners."

I forgot all that when I grew up. I trapped myself in a bad relationship. He hit me and our two kids when he drank. He broke all our dishes and then would start on us. I stayed with him for four years until I had enough. But I felt too scared to leave.

One night the police came because he threw bottles out on the street, screaming and yelling. The neighbors called 911. "Do you have any place to go, lady?" The policeman loomed over me with a too loud voice.

I froze. "No, I don't."

The cop shifted his hands from his gun to his nightstick. "We can only hold him for twenty-four hours and then he can return here."

Then some guys from the youth group passed by the house and came in. "Don't worry, we'll take care of you." They called up friends from our group. They laughed and joked around until six teens milled around the living room. Arron arrived and hugged me. "It's okay. We'll figure something out."

I just sat on a chair, afraid to speak. Soon the youth are packing up my stuff, finding a friend's truck, and getting directions. I smell fear in my sweat. I hold my crying kids on my lap. They have dirty clothes and don't smell too clean. My shoulder hurt and blood trickled from my mouth.

"Don't worry. It'll be okay." The guys kept saying this. I tried to smile but my face froze in a ragged line.

All that night the youth called people and pulled in favors to find me a safe place. Kaze, our youth missioner, arrived and pulled out her notebook with emergency numbers.

She looked at her list. "Okay, we can take you to a family safe house ninety miles from here that takes battered women and children. Do you want to do this? It means not coming back or telling him where you live. It gives you some space to think this through. We will support you regardless of your decision."

Everyone goes silent. I twisted my hands to stop shaking. I feel the blood dried on my face like a malignant growth. Someone reached for my hand to hold. I clutched it tightly. My mouth felt scratchy. I can't say anything. The decision stuck in my throat. I started crying which started my kids crying again.

My daughter pulled on my arm. "Mommy, let's go away." My little boy sniffled. I hate to see them hurting. My brain shouted at me to decide.

I hear my grandmother in my head: "Be strong in your roots. Never forget your kin." Her straight back and determined smile fills my space.

My head cleared up and I heard myself say, "Let's go."

It has been difficult, but I now have a good paying job. I keep my location secret but I'm in a safe apartment with two bedrooms. My night community college courses make my head swim with purpose. Best of all I reconnect to my family and pass on our cultural stories to my kids. I have some bad moments when I start sweating and go rigid with memories but I have worked through my past imprisonment. My children run in and out of the apartment with laugher rather than fear. I have planted new strong roots.

Contemplation Exercise, Boulder, CO.

SECTION TWO
Reclaiming Stories to Restore Dignity

"I believe much trouble would be saved if we opened our hearts more."

—Chief Joseph

La Verne, CA

Reclaiming Stories to Restore Dignity

"My grandmother told me the stories of the first people," Danny says. "She would put aside her wool and pick me up with her wrinkled hands. 'Show respect for the land people like wolf and the badger and the water people like the frog and the turtle.' She ended her stories by holding our head very still. 'Give thanks every day for all that has been given and show respect to everything from Mother Earth to Father Sky even if it is a rock.' I think about that a lot. Giving thanks and showing respect makes a good religion."

"Why do so many people say that they don't believe in God?" asks Natalie pushing her hair out of her face. We sit on the benches at a Winslow park, looking at the lone tree and patches of grass.

"They have forgotten that they are a part of an ancient story" I say. "Maybe they evade being filled with something awesome. What do you all think?"

Jake shakes his head. "I feel sorry for them. They make decisions by themselves. about how they feel and what they do by themselves. They aren't connected to others in a significant way or to the deep urges inside them. They don't see beauty or harmony or balance. They don't have a story to hold on to. To not know your people or have a story that connects you seems very sad. There is no starting place without a story."

On our journey we mold stories to inject coherence in our circumstances. Immediate concerns involve coping with highly charged encounters – fear, pain, grief, or rage. Some conversations carve a way to look at alternatives rather than feeling victimized by fate. Other dialogues expand our immediate worries to a larger picture. We keep inventing ways to tell a story in which we can own ourselves.

Three elements emerged which we illustrated in the following fifteen stories.

Three Story Elements:

1. Managing Issues

2. Affirming Life

3. Expanding Scope

1 Managing Issues

Discovering options on handling painful times.

"Isn't suicide an option?" asks Wally.

I don't know if Wally is depressed and/or serious. It makes no difference. If anyone mentions dying, the subject has to be addressed. "For me, suicide closes all options. What has to happen that you would close off any choices for something different?"

"Sometimes I just feel like dying would be better than hurting," says Wally.

"How have you handled your hurting before?" I ask.

Wally tears up. "When I was younger, I used to go pound something, like the wall. I'm glad I have my music. Writing songs helps me to not feel so bad. I guess I still want choices, but I wish it didn't hurt so much."

2 Affirming Life

Seeing possibilities in diverse situations.

"Everything is going wrong. I wish I lived somewhere else," says Mike.

"Do you think that will make a difference?" says Edwin. "No matter where you go, you still have to go through it. Sometimes you even find the good in it."

"Like what?" Mike asks.

"Like looking for new things you can do instead of bitching about it. You have to start with believing that something good can emerge. You can't start with dissing everything."

3 Expanding Scope

Broadening the range of decisions.

"Having to take 8th grade over again is the worst thing that ever happened to me," says Diana.

"What did you think?" asks Chris. "You skipped classes and never did any homework. Did you expect something else?"

"I thought it would work itself out," says Diana.

Chris shrugs, "You have to look at a larger picture. If you want to get out of Holbrook and get a job, and have something more, you have to look at what you want and what you have to do to get it. You can't just drift without knowing where you want to go."

Stories present a backdrop. A story weaves disparate and contradictive elements into a storyline that makes sense of whatever happens. If your story says that you always get the short end of the stick, then no matter what happens you respond as a victim to bad luck. If your story describes you on a journey, then whatever happens fits into that journey.

Youth Group, Holbrook, AZ

FIVE STORIES THAT REFLECT MANAGING ISSUES

Story 1: Transform Pain

In 2004 I visit Sammy in jail. His movements are jerky as he sits in his chair. "It's unfair. I defended myself from drunks when I left work. I retaliated with a screwdriver so they charge me for assault with a weapon."

The next week after the judge postpones his trial date for the fourth time, he tries to hang himself with a towel. They cut him down and put him into solitary confinement for the usual twenty-four hours.

Reclaiming Stories to Restore Dignity

When I receive permission to see him, he wears an orange jumpsuit and sits in a straight back chair. The guard who accompanies him sits at the other end of the room with an impassive face. Sammy keeps turning his head to check him out. He turns back to whisper. I can hardly hear him. "I couldn't see another way out. It hurts so much to be here. At least if I die, I won't hurt anymore. I can't stand being so alone."

How many times have I heard a teen say, "At least, if I kill myself, I will have done something? I can't stand it going on and on."

Teens often experience an event as the best thing or the worst thing that ever happens. The middle way doesn't seem to exist. Neither does the understanding that our emotional response to events can change.

Too many times I have met with Native youth who attempt suicide either at home or when incarcerated. Unmitigated pain without a story of change drives suicide.

If a constant drama of violence and belittling happens, youth often cannot see their anguish diminishing. Some may try cutting themselves to create a pain that they can control. Others react in outward violence to contain the hurt within. Some withdraw into a cocoon that insulates them from potential hurt. And some attempt suicide.

Healing requires techniques that manage pain. In the group we ask, "What has worked in the past?" They remember the solutions that have worked instead of the dead ends of their imagined future.

The Leadership Core (a small group in the Spirit Journey Youth) practice skills they want the younger teens to learn. We role-play familiar situations that seem to have no end. We start with "running away from home." Each writes down their suggested dialogue. We turn to our usual format for learning by playacting some familiar scenes.

Chuck, as the designated leader, begins by acknowledging the suffering.

"That sucks big time," he says. "I don't know how you stood it for so long."

For his second step he puts the issue on a continuum of suffering.

"Is it more about being put down or something like an ache that eats you from the inside or something else?"

Timmy, playing the runaway, says, "It's like I can't run fast enough to get far enough away."

The leader progresses to the next level of questions.

"What works for you when it all gets to be too much? What do you turn to?"

"I guess playing my guitar," he says. "It helps me forget, especially when I am learning a different kind of fingering. I find I can create something that sounds beautiful. I feel like I'm capable of doing one thing good."

This role play ends but the examples keep emerging. Sharon says, "I write poetry when I am down. It opens up so many things." We reflect on how our story changes when we can do something creative. Then we hone our questions to be used in future meetings.

Jake flops on the floor. "I like that we ask what is already working rather than offering advice on what they should do. This gives them control as well as reminding them that there has been a way out in bad times."

Years later, youth tell me they have used this to find within themselves a resource that handles their pain. They also tell me that it remains difficult.

Types and levels of pain change but how we manage it forms a defining story.

Story 2: Learning Trust

The cell phone rings late at night. My heart races. Is someone dead or hurt? I reach for the phone and my glasses at the same time. Rafe's voice keeps rising. "Can you come and get me. I'm in trouble." I dress, jump into my car and rush to Winslow street. Rafe has dried blood on his shirt and bruises on his face. We drive to an all-night café for coffee. No one else is there so we pick a back booth and make ourselves comfortable.

"I thought he was my friend but when I went to his house after I had been jumped, he wouldn't let me in." His eyes close tight. Bruises of contrasting colors speckle his face.

I place my hands on the table. "What did you expect of him?"

He glares. "I expected him to let me sleep there."

I hesitate, not meeting his eyes. "Do you have friends who will rescue you in the middle of the night?"

Rafe clears his throat. "If not, they won't be my friends."

"I remember when I expected friends to be totally trustworthy and listen to me complain," I say. "They kept disappointing me by either being patronizing or judgmental. My older sister told me 'You will probably only trust one or two people totally throughout your life. I trust some people with finances but not to pick me up when I have car trouble at 2 a.m. I trust some with my kids' lives but not with food shopping. I learn to trust people with those things in which they can be trustworthy and accept others in their imperfection. Just as I want them to trust me.'"

"Yes," I say. "It helped. I learned about accepting people as they are."

We both turn around at the noise as four members of our youth group walk toward us. They greet us with surprise. Nick says "What are you guys doing here? We just finished a super video game."

The booth shudders as the youth flop on the benches. Rafe says "Trust. We're talking about who we can trust."

Ken says "I can talk about that. I don't believe very many people can be trusted. I get jerked around all the time."

I step in. "Before we talk about all our examples of distrust, tell me when you want trust."

The five teens poured out their examples: "I want to trust that people who know intimate things about me won't gossip or use it against me." "I want to trust that I can reveal bad things about myself without being judged." "I want to trust that someone has my back." "I want to trust that a friend will be kind to me even when I don't deserve it."

Rafe says, "It's complicated. I guess that trust is a two-way street with lots of levels. I'm not sure how to find out from others what they trust in me. Or how to show a little appreciation for those I depend on, especially my girl."

In minuscule moves, Ken adjusts his ball cap. "Most of my disappointments involve trusting the wrong person or the wrong thing. If I don't crawl into a hole and live only by myself, then I have to figure out how to trust smarter. I just don't know how to do that."

Danny speaks up. "I remember when I really needed a friend to talk to but I was afraid he would make fun of me or tell somebody else. Finally, he told me to stop wasting his time and just tell him what is going on. I felt like he was asking me to rip my guts out and lay them on the table. I finally just blurted it out. Talk about vulnerability. I didn't think I could ever look him in the eyes."

"So, what happened?" asks Rafe.

"He became my best friend. We tell each other everything. My story changed. If I wanted to be trusted, I had to risk trusting."

"Let's talk about this again," says Ken. "I've got a headache with all this thinking."

We laugh and agree to talk both about vulnerability and trusting in future meetings. We troop out of the café with the teens jostling each other and joking. I feel a sense of hope as I drag myself back into the car and go home to bed.

Story 3: Dislodging Habits

We sit in the swing outside the community center, shivering a little from the wind. Nick talks about his history with drinking. "By the time I turned eight, my mom let me finish off the end of her beer. I picked up her matches on the kitchen table and started burning things. When I tried to burn down the bridge downtown, the police arrested me and called Social Services. They dismissed me with a warning. I never did stop drinking."

"Do you want to?" I ask.

"Yeah," he says. "I've tried, but I always fall back."

Other youth wander over to the swing to listen. Sherry pushes her hair back. "So, are we going to talk about getting rid of bad habits?"

"I guess so," I say. "Let's go into the community center."

As we find pillows to sit on, I remember the many times I've witnessed destructive ingrained habits. Drinking in America typically starts at nine-years old. Drug use follows when they reach eleven. These ingrained habits do not help in obtaining a job in mainstream society or establishing stable relationships. As I look at these at-risk teens, their need to change built-in behaviors stays paramount for their growth.

Rafe shares memories about some of their bad behaviors. "Remember when Wally used to demand you stop the van for a crap stop."

Everyone snickers at the crudity. "You kept telling him to ask for a pit stop. He really did not understand the difference. Finally, we all started correcting him until we laughed so hard we all had to stop at the next rest stop. I don't think he ever understood the difference but he did change and he laughed with us."

Lisa says, "I remember how many times you told us not to pick up things we found in our host's house or church and put it into our pockets. At first, we thought you were really strange. After our third trip in someone else's home, we started mimicking you. 'Don't walk away when someone is talking to you. Don't turn on the TV or radio without asking permission. Thank your hostess for inviting you. Keep your phone in your pocket.' I think we finally got it."

"Alright," I say, also laughing at the memory. "Let's make a list of new habits you want to install in yourself. Name the habits that stop you from being employable or anything that has you responding reactively, like fighting."

The list they make include: *Keep my promise; finish what I start; learn new things; walk away from fighting; apologize when I am wrong; stand up to a bully; stop drinking and using; have a purpose; use polite language; pray more; and have courage to say what I think.*

"Just saying I'm going to change does not change me. I've been there too many times." Sammy shakes his shoulders as if he wants to throw off something.

"Okay," I say. "Instead of talking about our failures, let's talk about when we need change. We may find some new things we can try."

They list some scenes in which they would like some different endings: "I wake up at night and hear the adults shouting at each other. They sound drunk. Usually I yell at them." "He pulls a knife on me and calls me a loser. I fight back." "The cool guys at school push a little guy around and call him names. I ignore it." "My brother brings drugs into our home and I get punished for it. They are yelling at me and I can't stand it. They start punching me. I punch back."

We decide to role-play these scenes. This become cathartic as we work out some of the more painful experiences. Emotions spill over.

Sometimes we role play the same scene repeatedly to establish new behavior. Anger, hurt, and justification pour out of the teens as they relive painful memories in which their responses only made their situation worse.

The scene they repeat the most includes this situation: "They start punching me. I hit back. I'm filled with rage and violence."

Confidence increases as we practice habits we want to install. We create short sentences to remember the habits we have chosen. "Stick to it." "Apologies increase my power." "Give it up." "Only one day at a time." "Compassion rules." We laugh at how inane it sounds.

Rafe shakes his head. Most of our advice to ourselves is how to stop doing something. Making a list of friends we call when it gets too much seems more practical. I need help to change from the inside."

I pace up and down as I struggle to find some wisdom. "Changing the environment in which these old habits emerge works. If you drink or use with your friends at the park, change your friends or don't go to the park. Avoid situations of violence if possible. Practice speaking up rather than ignoring things. You have to find practical alternatives for yourself."

The youth look at me with mixed expressions on their faces. I'm not sure if they feel hopeless or reassured. "You may consider expanding your council of friends."

Lisa bounces to her feet. "I don't understand."

I settle back against the wall. "Choose to remember particular people who will back you in the behavior you want. Pick one who encourages you, one who accepts you no matter what, and one who pushes you to try new things. When you find yourself falling back into habits of fear and violence, call on your council."

Wally pounds the table, "It sounds stupid but I'll try it. I have to change. Everything I do just gets me in more trouble. I don't want to have to go to juvie again. I don't want to have to go to school with a bruised face. I don't want to hate myself for being so weak that all I can do is fight blindly. I want the strength to remember this."

"I hate to fight all the time," says Danny. "My grandmother told me self-control is my heritage; respect is my creed. She's on my council. And so is the youth group. When we get together, we believe we can be more than past mistakes."

During the year, we talk about our councils. They usually chose a grandparent, a boy or girl friend and a best friend or a teacher. The youth tell me that it becomes easier to not fight or drink or run away but they need to recall their council often.

We make it a part of our regular exercise to act out some of the new ways we want to respond and look confident and if possible, cool and safe. It cements us as a group as we realize how much we need mutual support to focus us.

Story 4: Ego Trip

Earl Gibson, a youth minister in California calls me "Why don't you have your kids help at the Vacation Bible School for a week. It will teach them some new skills and maybe help them to socialize."

I don't agree. I think the youth will rebel against helping kids from a well-to-do neighborhood. But the kids say yes, with conditions.

Folding their arms, they present their stipulations. "We will only work with the older kids. We are not going to baby sit a bunch of Anglos."

After a twelve-hour drive we arrive at Saint John's in La Verne. The Vicar, Kelli Grace explains the system. "You have to put your ego aside. You will be singing silly songs and helping those younger than you to do uncool things Are you willing to do this?"

I hold my breath. They don't want to work with younger kids.

Surprisingly they all say "Yes."

She makes the assignments to the different age groups. I hold my breath again.

She points to the toughest "cool" leader who has already spent time in juvenile detention. "You have the Butterflies, the youngest group."

My breathing stops. Jake cannot possibly agree to work with this silly, uncool name.

He hesitates. Then he says, "Okay, Go Butterflies!"

We all laugh and I wonder how this miracle happened. For the week, "setting aside our egos" becomes our watchword.

When we return to Arizona, we keep this skill of setting aside "cool" for the sake of something bigger.

In November, Danny takes me aside with a proposal. "Let's collect some coats and blankets for the homeless who live under the bridge. Our group can ask around for donations. We know a lot of people."

To my surprise, the youth filled twelve black garbage bags. We meet at the bridge.

Della asks, "I don't think I can do this. What if they act crazy?"

I look around and notice that the teens who have not been on our trips looking at each other. I lean over to whisper to Danny. "I think they need a reason why we do this.

Danny gives this story, "Sometimes we do something that makes us uncomfortable like talking with homeless people who may be drunk or crazy. I know for me, when my family lived on the streets, I hated people treating me like a poor charity case. So we need to be different. We are going to put aside our egos and not act like someone superior just because we have a house. We will act like their sons and daughters giving back, treating them with great respect."

Sammy shifts weight from one foot to the other. "But what if someone from our school sees us? They will call us "god boys."

Others laugh nervously.

Danny looks carefully at the youth standing in front of him. "That's what putting our ego aside means. We do whatever it takes to make the homeless comfortable. We can't think about our being cool. It's not about us."

After a discussion, everyone decides to try it.

That evening remains a signal event for our youth group. We give coats, sweaters, beanies, socks and gloves. We laugh and talk with the street people and we find connections among the homeless, with each other and with something holy.

Ken, who has just turned thirteen, sums it up: "I've been worrying about the wrong thing I think. This is so strange to not care about what others think. Maybe this is the new cool?"

Story 5: Stepping Back

"I don't know why I get so caught up in drama," Edwin blurts out. Five of us sit in our usual booth in a diner talking through the latest 'incident." We jostle each other as we reach for condiments that seem to live under someone's elbow.

Edwin blows on his coffee to cool it. "I always react by jumping out of my skin half way to the door. I wish I could be calm and say something smart for once."

The teens exchange stories of their impulsive reactions to stressful situations. Self-condemnations litter the conversation. Zach shivers. "I feel so stupid sometimes."

An almost inaudible sound comes out of my throat. They look at me. I manage to breathe deeply and casually scan the group. "We can all get caught in a box of first reactions," I start. "Fortunately, we can stand back and choose how we want to respond rather than just jumping in."

"How do you do that?" asks Edwin. "I just freeze up or run. Sometimes I start stuttering."

I carefully arrange my words in my mind. "Somehow we get caught in our guilt. Maybe we label something as factual (I'm about to be hit) rather than recognizing that we are interpreting the situation (Her voice is getting really loud and I know what that means.)"

The four youth wait patiently for me to explain more.

I give an example. "My boss raises her voice at me and I want to run away. I have already interpreted the scene as bad and my best choice reduced to running. But I have another option. I can physically take a step back. This takes it out of my head and my body responds without my brain connecting. By taking a physical step back, I go from inside to out. That helps me think of other alternatives; like taking a walk, or talking things out, or standing next to someone else. It takes a lot of practice to choose how I want things to go rather than being ruled by fear."

We go outside to practice. Arron yells at Zach. He flinches and then remembers to step back. Arron yells again. This time Zach takes two steps back and breathes deeply.

Zach looks at the others. "It works. I can feel my panic leave my brain and disappear into my feet. How awesome!"

Edwin says "You hit it on target about the guilt. I hate myself as a quitter and a coward who runs away. I keep making the situation worse. Maybe we can practice a little bit more."

We practice some more. Each one thinks of an emotional situation when panic fills the brain and thoughts cycle endlessly. George play acts how he usually responds by bitter words. "I want to stop myself from mouthing off. I hate myself when I say something mean just because I'm afraid I might get hurt." He practices stepping back and even sideways. Everyone takes a turn in practicing.

Arron says "When I don't panic, I realize that I misinterpreted the situation. I didn't get hurt. It was just a bad moment. I remember when I first learned that there is no such thing as just 'reality.' When we interpret what we see and hear, more than one explanation can emerge. It has changed my story of how I can manage bad things."

Edwin dances from one foot to the other. "This is so cool. I can do this. I wish I had known this before I got into fights."

We all laugh and think of our own "wish I had known this in the past."

FIVE STORIES THAT REFLECT AFFIRMING LIFE

Story 6: Core Identity

Two of the youth sit in a corner of the community room. They keep kicking the floor with their shoes like they wish the floor had a face. They verbally bait each other with words like "Loser" and "Quitter." They end up shouting to each other, "You suck." This echoes throughout our space. They drift toward my table.

Hank says to them, "Do you really want those words to define you? Those labels sound so silly."

This begins a conversation on what defines us. We gather around the table munching on pizza. "So, what really explains your uniqueness?" I ask. "What if you lost something important, would you still be you? How would you ask the question?"

Wally begins, "If I lose my leg, am I someone else?" Others make up questions: "If you lose your girlfriend, how do you talk about yourself?" "If you lose your job, are you different?" "If you lose your language and forget your ceremonies, do you stop being Native?"

Hank says, "I think our identity changes when we lose something important. There has to be a core me but I don't know what that means."

At the nods from the group, I ask, "When someone talks about you, what do they treasure about you?"

This time the responses come quickly.

"They know I am Navajo (or Hopi or Kiowa).

"They know that I help people and share what I have."

"They know I have their back, no matter what."

"What else am I?" asks Wally. "That doesn't seem enough."

Sensing that they are on a roll, I ask "What keeps you going in dark times?" Sammy turns his head side to side repeatedly. "I hate it when people only see me as shallow. When I sing along with my guitar I can recognize me as *me*."

Ken drums his fists on the table. "Now that you ask the question, I see myself standing under a waterfall feeling more alive than ever. I am a lot more than people see."

"I draw all the time," says Drew. "I doodle a lot but sometimes I really draw something deep and I feel gigantic like I float among the stars."

We talk about identity for several weeks. At the beginning of one of our Sunday meetings, Hank says, "I have been thinking about this a lot. I am defined by my Natives stories. Those stories of being kept alive by my respect of Mother Earth and Father Sky allows me to see the sacred in the smallest things."

No one has anything more to say. For the time being, everyone sprawls in different directions. As I look around, their uniqueness seems obvious. Hank chews things over and over until he shares an idea with the others. Wally never gives up until he finds a solution. Drew looks and finds the extraordinary in his art.

The story of our identity establishes itself not in what we do or what we have but in what keeps us going below the surface.

Story 7: Comprehensive View

"Look at the big picture," snorts Les. "That's what she tells me to do. What a waste of time to go to counseling."

The courts assign him to anger management. He waits outside the counselor's office standing up and sitting down repeatedly. "I hate being lectured by the same old things."

I wait with him, sitting on the hard chairs of the office. I turn to Les. "When I was your age, I could not see beyond the pain of my situation. I had to learn how to go beyond the particular. As I began my sobriety journey twenty-five years ago, I followed the platitude of 'do the next good thing.' I learned to think only of the very next step. But one day when my anger erupted at a trivial incident, I began to look beyond the next step, to see the whole. I forced myself to look at all the things to which I am connected. This made me see implications beyond the immediate"

Les' eyes open wide. "What did you do? Do you still do it?"

I chuckle at his eagerness. "I usually take a legal pad and pencil and draw lines to all my connections. For a long time, I belonged to one organization that works in global village communities. When I left the group, I feared that I would end up behind a desk doing irrelevant stuff. I kept finding more and more connections. I finished with pages of people I know, things I could do, places I could live and dreams I still had. I wrote down what I wanted to become as a person, as a member of my family, as a Church member, as a teacher, as a hard worker, as a mentor, and as a spiritual writer. I considered places and roles that would allow me to continue to dwell in the sacred. I had so many lines it looked like a spider web. I put circles around the important ones. Then I sketched stick figures of giraffes and youth in the circles. This broke my paralysis."

He laughs with me and starts thinking aloud. "That might work. I have to consider my younger brother and my family and maybe my future. I never thought of it before. I can draw. Maybe I can paint all the different places and things I want to do. Maybe I can draw me in different expressions. It's not just about me. My brother and relatives are going to be looking at what I become. I connect to a lot of things that I don't think about much."

The counselor appears and Les goes into her office. I sit and marvel at how much we achieved in one hour. I impatiently wait for Les to return so we can talk more about connections and possibilities.

Several months later, Les drops by to talk. "It's very strange. In these last two months, I have talked more to my family than I have ever done before. I have even gone to the Rez to see people I have ignored for years. Now the garbage that used to block me doesn't seem so impossible anymore. My grandmother always told me that as long as I respect my relations, I will know who I am. I don't want to go back to who I used to be."

I reassure him and myself. "Once we go beyond, we can't shrink back to a single circle."

Story 8: Yes and No

Lisa and I sit in discreet shadows in the café's back booth. Two of her friends join us as we talk. Lisa tells me, "Nothing I do earns praise or even tepid approval. I get punished for being too quiet or too loud. Look at these cigarette burns she gave me on my arm. I brought home an 'A' on my essay. My stepmother told me I was too proud. I get labeled no matter what I do."

She tears up as she looks down at her hands. "No matter what I do, it's bad and I am going to hell. It's evil. There is no good in living at home. I hate the drinking and the violence and living with fear. I hate their judgment, their punishments, and their dislike of me. If I had my own baby someone would love me as I am."

"You have every right to be disgusted with all of this." I try to modulate my tone so she cannot hear my anguish. "We can work on changing things for you." I stand up abruptly as the cruelty of her story overwhelms me.

"I can't get over how much damage I give back to everyone." She bows her head with her fists clenched.

Taking a calming breath, I work to stay objective. "We all condemn ourselves sometimes. Intense words like 'evil and good' cause instant self-judgment They label us with exaggerated flaws or expectations."

Betty raises her eyebrows. "So what else can we say."

"Yes and No," I say. "Sometimes I get praised so I give that a big 'Yes.' Sometimes a giant slam in the face tears me down so I say, 'No.' They both inform me. The importance lies not in a pat on the head or a kick in the butt, but in what lets me go forward."

"How do you do that?" asks Sherry.

"I think about the yes and no possibilities in whatever happens." I stare at my coffee, hoping adequate words will emerge. "If I call it good or evil, then I judge myself and muddle my mind with guilt or pride. It polarizes me into thinking I am either good or bad."

Breathing deeply, I continue. "Lisa, you told me that they called you a loser and made some impossible demands. How do you see both the 'yes' and the 'no' in this for you?"

She takes a few minutes to reflect. "The 'no' is that I know what is bad and what I don't want in my life anymore. The 'yes' is that I have a way out by staying in school until I can leave home at eighteen. I just have to figure out how I can stand it for that long."

Betty claps her hands. "Let's practice some more. My boyfriend yells at me at little stuff. Then he whispers sweet things to me and apologizes for getting mad."

"So, what's the 'yes' and 'no' for you?" I ask.

"The 'yes' is easy. He knows I get upset when he yells so we need a way to talk about it when he is calm. The 'no' is that we both get too upset to think about anything when he gets angry and I start crying."

I ask, "What do you learn from this?"

Betty says, "Maybe I can suggest that we both get too emotional when things don't go our way so we can create a time out when it happens. I cry and he yells. We could each stand against the wall until we quiet down. I wonder if this could work?"

We laugh with her as we think of her six-foot tall boyfriend standing against a wall. "Does this 'yes' and 'no' exercise help?"

Lisa says, "It works for me. I can look for what I can do rather than how bad I am. I didn't think it would work."

With that, we pack up our stuff and leave the café. Sherry says, "Let's do this again with the whole group. The boys need to learn this too."

As I drive away, I enjoy the results of going beyond polarizing labels and learning what can move us forward. I look back at the girls with hope and trepidation that society's crushing judgments on them will trickle away with each yes and no.

Story 9: Healing Sage

Twelve of our youth group gather at the Hozhoni Center (our drop in center in Holbrook). Some play pool and others enjoy video games. Gene walks in with hunched shoulders and misery etched in the lines of his forehead. He shoves some of the younger kids around and yells obscenities at us. Backed by two of the older youth, we persuade him to go outside while the rest of us sit in a circle on the floor.

"How shall we handle this?" I look around at the sitting youth

Drew jerks his head back. "Why ask us? We have rules. Kick him out."

Arron disagrees, "He's one of us."

We sit for a while. Finally, I stand up. "This has become a Native peer issue. Some of you can talk to the young ones bullied by Gene and others can talk to Gene. It's not about rules. It's about what will keep the future open for everyone concerned. Adults in authority don't carry any weight. You know best how to speak to the situation."

I retreat into the kitchen for coffee as they form two groups to talk about this.

Arron asks me for the eagle feather and sage we keep in a special box. I get them and return to the kitchen.

They talk in earnest to the young ones who have been bullied and still have the shakes.

Others go out to find Gene and bring him back inside.

They call me back in and I sit in the circle with them. Arron smudges everyone with sage pronouncing the words to "walk in beauty."

They tell stories from their grandparents about the importance of controlling anger and protecting the vulnerable. Wally says, "My grandmother told me that our pride in being Native is how we respect others, especially children and old people."

"My grandmother used to say 'All we have is our honor. Everything else can be taken away from us,'" says Ken.

Very carefully, several mention the times they had messed up and how they regained their balance. No one makes any demands. Several youth promise the frightened kids that they have their back and will keep them safe.

We all wait. Gene stares down at his hands, not saying a word.

Arron silently hands the eagle feather and sage to Gene. His face contorts and his body stiffens. Finally, he shudders, and takes the feather and sage as though he remembers this Native tradition from ancient times. He walks around the circle blessing everyone with the sage.

No words break the silence.

Later, Ken tells me that no one ever asks for their opinion. "I feel bigger because you left it with us."

A kind of reconciliation happened with the assumption of responsibility in the circle and the sage. It restores and empowers us.

Story 10: Claiming a Promise

For many in this at-risk youth group, birthdays are only celebrated when they are small children. Most never have a cake with their name on it or candles that count the years.

Hearing comments from Sammy about feeling invisible, I suggest a community celebration on his birthday.

The youth group comes together for a party at the Hozhoni youth center. We shopped together for balloons, a cake, and a gift of a new shirt. "Cool," says Rafe looking around the room. "I didn't think this gloomy place could look so good."

As we bring in the cake with lighted candles, Sammy's eyes fixate on the cake. We start joking with each other to avoid looking at his moist eyes.

Rafe exaggerates his sniffing the cake. "Blow out the candles. Make a wish Dude."

We fall quiet as he just stares at the cake. He clears his throat several times. "I've never seen my name on a cake before." Carefully he traces his name that is written in frosting on the cake. He blows out the candles. "I wish I stay alive to celebrate my seventeenth birthday."

His pronouncement has the group coughing to clear throats.

Rolland whispers to me "Do we say something nice about him now?"

Not sure just what kind of compliments he might receive, I dip into a question I remember from my Chicago days as a community developer.

"Let's claim a promise for him." I smile, as I remember this being asked me at my surprise fortieth birthday party in Kenya.

Blank stares greet me. "What?"

"It means that you see something important growing in a person and you want the person to reach for it," I say.

"You mean a wish, like lots of girls?" suggests Rafe. He grins. "That's what he needs."

Everyone laughs.

"Not that," I say. "Say something that connects to Sammy, something important that you want him to reach for."

They look at me like I have gone gaga.

"Okay." I push my hair off my forehead. "Someone claimed a promise for me years ago that I would put my insights into written words. Up to that time, I gave lectures and presentations. I did not write. Sharing my writing scared me but someone saw a promise in me that stretched beyond my comfort zone. Much later, in my 60's, another friend suggests that I write stories. Now I write all the time. The promise finally claimed me."

The youth make some superficial but funny promises. "I claim that he grows taller than his brother." "I claim that he gives back my shirt."

Finally, Hank speaks up. "I'll try it. He really shows compassion to his younger siblings when they get hurt. I claim the promise that he extends his consideration to those beyond his immediate family."

Silence reigns for a moment. "Wow!" Sammy opens his eyes wide. "That's deep. Maybe I can."

Sherry looks at me directly. "I've got one. I claim the promise that you stop apologizing when you say something smart and just accept that you have a brain."

The teens nod their heads.

Sammy straightens up in his chair and grins as the youth point out other positive character traits. Since that afternoon the kids tell me how they have shaped their stories to include promises that challenge them. By empowering Sammy, we empower ourselves.

FIVE STORIES THAT REFLECT EXPANDING SCOPE

Story 11: Gaining Substance

Our van with seven seats remains the place for fruitful conversations. We drive to Parker, Arizona for a Native meeting. Wrappers of snack food and plastic bottles litter the floor. We stop frequently to walk around or eat, talking incessantly about every imaginable subject. On this trip, compulsions top our list of concerns.

These teenagers see from a specialized viewpoint; a survival trait for those surrounded with violence and driven by poverty. Eating everything in sight, spending money at once and swiftly responding to viciousness remains driven by impulse. They often react rather than plan.

"You should have seen me dive through the door to get away from my stepfather's fist." Buddy throws his head back, letting his long black hair swing. "I'm getting really fast."

Laughter ripples through the van. Buddy continues, "I just wish I could figure out how to avoid my stepfather in the first place."

As the kids discuss this, I remember how often they become frozen on the superficial level in dramatic situations. They continue skimming the surface rather than looking deeper.

When we arrive back home in Northern Arizona, I take each teen to their home. Later, four of the youth come by my studio apartment and ask about improving their way of responding to drama. I invite them in and we all find somewhere to sit.

"I hate seeing my little brother cry." Chuck looks down at his hands. "We had a lot of drama last night and he got roughed up. He doesn't understand that he has to stand tough if he wants to survive. He's got to get used to a lot more drama and a lot more s**t."

We stay quiet, looking at each other.

Zach looks straight at him. "I hope he doesn't get used to it. I hope that he finds another way to live. He doesn't have to be stuck in this."

The other kids nod.

"I'm getting away from all this." Wally says. He flexes his tattoos up and down his arms. "I want a life that's different, where I don't have to run away all the time or lie about what happens at home. Life in this town is so flat."

I look at the young faces around me. "How can you make this possible?"

Zach tilts back his chair with a grin spread over his face. "You told us once to look for more and not get hooked by the surface stuff. I remember that."

He continues, "I think of the times you ask, 'What did you learn from this?' What is sacred in that? Or what did your grandparents teach you? I try to look for something bigger, something I could reach for. It keeps me sane in the dark times."

"How do you do that?" Wally asks.

Zach fiddles with his baseball cap. "I look at myself as I have become. Before we started our mission trips, I thought of myself stuck in this town with no future. Now I think about California or New York and all the people I've met. I could live anywhere and there is a whole world out there where I could work and find a different life."

His grin fades. "I used to think I couldn't handle hard stuff; that I could just drift. Now, I don't know, I feel like I have a bigger mind. But sometimes it hurts to think hard."

"Is that enough?" asks Chuck. "We just have to think big?"

"No," says Zach. "It's about going places, meeting people, doing new things. It's about all the things that push us to think. It gets us out of 'stuck' in the fast lane."

As they file out the door, Chuck says "Sounds right to me. I hate being stuck. Let's go somewhere."

Reclaiming Story 12: Choosing Integrity

The youth group sits in a circle at a friend's house in Boulder. It is our first mission trip to Colorado. The host family serves us pizza on our arrival. The home features a long couch and a wide rug space. Drew shifts the cushion on the floor around several times. "Do you like people who achieve something?"

"Of course," I laugh. "But I mainly like those who live down-to-earth. What do you like?"

"I like rich people," he says with a big grin. Everyone laughs.

As we chomp on pepperoni pizza, Timmy asks, "What if you found a bundle of money with no identification and nobody knows about it. Would you keep it?"

I hesitate, freezing my facial features.

He jumps on it. "Ha, I knew you would keep it."

I still hesitate. Everyone giggles.

"Shut up and let her think," commands Arron pushing up his sleeves.

I think aloud. "You are asking me about honesty. That word doesn't hold it for me. I don't make decisions based on whether or not someone can catch me."

"What word would you use?" asks Arron.

"Integrity," I say.

"I remember when you complained about the store manager automatically distrusting you. He followed us around the store just daring you to steal something. We talked about how you could be seen as honorable. We learn how to be authentic; to make real choices to do the right thing as we see it. Remember that time in Flagstaff when you gave up your lunch money to buy food for the homeless by the dumpster. That's integrity."

Monica says, "That's hard core. Does that mean we can never do anything dishonest?

"Anyone want to talk about this?" I ask the group.

Zach shifts around in his chair. "I do find myself thinking twice before I do something wrong now. I remember when my older brother took a job washing dishes to help pay for his kid. He was going to college but took a low paying job instead. I admired him for that. He stood up as a man when he found out about his kid. I want to be a stand-up guy too."

Timmy says, "I apologize for being a smart mouth. I know you would do the right thing and return the money. I know that you want us to be that way. Sometimes I don't think I can."

Arron stands up and starts pacing the floor. "When I was younger, teachers used to talk a lot about making good choices. That seemed impossible when every decision I made was criticized. I had to learn to be a strong Native as my grandmother taught me. I came home one day really angry at someone who stole my money at school. She said, 'Being strong means you don't posture or talk big. It means you make a decision to be dependable. If you get a girl pregnant you take responsibility for the money needed. If you mess up, you own up to it and stop making excuses. You don't take or give big talk. You talk respect.' When I was put in charge of the homeless lunches, I started to complain but decided to be grown up about it. That was the day when I decided to be responsible. I guess that began my journey of integrity."

The kids have been hanging on to Arron's every word. There seems to be nothing more to say, so we go into the kitchen for more pizza. Integrity requires a substantial commitment that we continue to explore.

Reclaiming Story 13: Blame Game

Sharon fills up her tea glass. "It's not my fault." We hold an all-girls meeting in the community hall to discuss relationship problems. A collective sigh ripples through the room at this protest of innocence.

"It doesn't work to focus on guilt or innocence," I say. "That causes weak boundaries."

Natalie jumps up from the sofa. "What do boundaries mean?"

"Boundaries protect us from intrusion; like an invisible wall we put around ourselves," I say. "We say 'No' to being abused and to being victims. We say 'Yes' to stable relationships. When we label ourselves guilty or innocent we erode our boundaries by playing the blame game. Instead of shielding ourselves, we find fault instead of drawing a line to protect our dignity."

Betty wraps her sweater around herself in a partial hug. "I've heard about boundaries. But I don't have the will power to stop someone stronger."

Her shoulders seem permanently wilted. "I don't even want to get up but I have to go to school so I drag myself around. I hate it when friends try to cheer me up. I can't afford to care what others feel. I know I'm bad. Others don't have to tell me."

Diana speaks so softly that we lean forward to hear. "I wish I didn't care. I cry all the time. Any time someone is mean to me, I start crying. I just keep saying 'I'm sorry,' even if I don't know what I am sorry about."

Others open up. Betty looks around before admitting, "I used to feel good about myself. Whenever he accuses me of being wrong, I feel that in my gut. I can't eat. I do so many wrong things. I feel guilty all the time."

I clear my throat. "That's the story you tell yourself. To have strong boundaries, you have to change your story. You can't let your emotional reactions trip you up."

I turn to Sharon who feels wrong whenever someone says, "It's your fault."

"If it is not your fault, what emerges as the real issue?" I ask.

Sharon hangs her head. "He wants me to read his mind. I don't know what he means when he glares at me. He wants me to know when he wants quiet and when he wants to eat. And I always guess wrong."

"How do we get beyond feeling guilty?" asks Diana.

I stand up at the chalk board. "Let's do a game called 'Drawing a Line.' We all have emotional and sometimes violent triggers that have us lose control. This line game has us step back from the emotion to hold on to our values. We start by listing our boundaries. What will you allow and not allow in this relationship?"

At first they giggle. Then they make a few tentative suggestions. "We don't discuss anything if either one of us is drunk." "He can't say his side without listening to mine." "He can't use past mistakes to justify what he wants." "We have to stick to the issue and not end up name calling."

I ask Sharon, "What's the line you have drawn in your relationship?"

"He's got to listen to me instead of blaming me," she says.

With these few but important boundaries in place, we role-play situations.

They imagine an invisible line drawn on the floor as their boundary. Sharon stands behind the line, crossing her arms consciously.

She yells "Don't blame me." With a half-smile she steps back. "I don't know what to do next."

The girls can't talk fast enough. "He wants to control you." "Ask him if he wants you to leave since it is always your fault." "No, ask him what the two of you can do to have a good life." "I think the issue is that he also has triggers. Maybe you can talk about it."

She unfolds her arms and continues the role play. "Okay, we both have sides. I want some space where I can think about things and we can talk about what's wrong. What do you want?"

We all applaud. Sharon blinks back tears. "It may not work but it doesn't seem so dark."

Beth says "I'm not sure what the issues are but it frees me to not get stuck in my own bulls**t."

"I live a lot of my life thinking how wrong I am," says Lisa. I used to fight when someone says it's my fault. Maybe it's not."

"Do you think these boundaries will last?" asks Beth.

Natalie says. "It will if we draw the line over and over again."

As we clean the tables and lock up the building, my heart fills with hope that the 'blame game' has been dealt a death blow.

Story 14: Past Shaping

The past keeps intruding.

Ken tells me about one event over and over. "He slaps my mother, glares at me and my two siblings and leaves, slamming the door. I didn't see him for another fifteen years."

At the first telling of this story, he wants the chance to beat up his father when he first sees him. "Just one punch, right in the face," he announces pounding his fist into his hand.

As he grows in confidence and purpose, he learns something different from the telling of it.

"I don't want to go to jail like my father," he declares, sitting up straight in his chair.

A few years later when we are having coffee, I notice that he now dresses in a good shirt and khaki pants. "I want my family to be proud of what I do. I don't want my brother and sister to grow up thinking they have to be like my father."

By the time he is eighteen his face has the lines of an adult. "I think my father leaving came as a wakeup call for me. I still decide what kind of man I want to be. I used to think that we got a raw deal when he left. Now, I think that I had to learn what the real world is like. It is up to me to be what I want."

I don't know how many more times he will change the lens through which he sees his past. Last week he told me, "I love our reflections at the end of our meetings, especially when we discuss what we learn from our experiences. I used to just let things happen to me and never think of how it affects me."

In small pieces, his story is informed as he integrates his history.

I go to sleep that night relieved at his growth.

The next morning Ken wakes me up with a report on two cousins fighting at his house. I get dressed and drive over at 4 a.m. The two cousins (Rolland and Glen) have blood over their shirts. Rolland has tears dripping down his face.

He tells me that Glen called him an "a**hole." He exploded and slams Glen's head into the ground repeatedly. He sobs. "I didn't even think. He calls me what my father and his brother used to call me and I jump in to kill him. I love my cousin. I don't want to hurt him. He doesn't know how to fight. Why do I do this?"

I sit between the cousins. "Some things that took place in an earlier time keep popping up and having us react in fear and violence. We have to reconcile our past so those triggers can no longer control us."

Ken twirls his baseball cap in his hands. "It's about the story. When I got hurt as a kid, I felt like a victim with no control over my anger. I lashed out at everyone. I finally got it together and announced that I was moving to another city to start over again. Before I left my younger brother took me aside. 'What about me?' he begged. 'You have to show me how to handle the drunks Mom brings home. You just can't run away and leave me here. At least you can get me a gun to defend myself.'"

I sat down hard on the living room couch. I told my brother "I don't roll that way anymore. I don't fight my way out every situation."

"My brother asks, "What else can I do but fight?"

Rolland asks, "What did you tell him?"

"I told him that I have a different story now of who I am," says Ken. "First I told him to forget the gun. I showed him how to go out the back window, how to cook for himself, and who to call."

"Why?" he asks.

"We have to look at what hurt us and put it alongside what we want to be in the future," says Ken. "It can be something that makes us determined or something we want to avoid. I want to have a family of my own that doesn't fight at everything; where I have a good job and we have enough food and clothes and a nice apartment. One thing I have learned is to unravel what used to happen in light of what I want my life to be."

The cousins look at each other and give each other an awkward hug. Rolland says, "I guess I need a new story too. I don't want to ever explode like that again. I don't want my past life to keep strangling me. How do I do this exactly?"

As I get up to leave I say, "Take Ken's advice. Look at what hurt you in the past and put it alongside what your purpose is now. You may be surprised at how your story of who you are changes."

Reclaiming Story 15: Knowing the Difference

"So what happened last night," I ask. Several Native youth slouch in their seats at the cafe with their baseball caps pulled over their eyes. They all look away when I question them.

George recounts the events. "A bunch of guys saw us walking down the street. They were looking for a fight and when they saw us they started staring us down. We didn't back down even though we didn't want to fight. They all looked like they could take us down. One of our guys said, 'What up?' They all responded, 'What up?" and nothing happened. We all walked away happy. It was close."

"Okay." I scan the group with soft eyes. "Name me the facts and your opinions. Remember factual means what you hear and see. Opinion means your interpretation of what you see and hear."

George looks down at his feet. "You didn't see them. They wanted to fight."

I sigh. "I want you to trust your feelings. Your survival depends on it. I also want you to be aware of your interpretations that sometimes may not be accurate. Humor me. What did you see on their faces that led you to believe they wanted to fight?"

Having done this exercise before, Henry smiles smugly. "Their mouths turned down in a frown and they squinted their eyes."

Nick twirls his cap in his hands and looks everywhere but at me. "Their eyes never left our faces and they walked slowly."

We proceed to the next phase. "Name a different interpretation of what you saw when they came toward you or when they stared?" I look over their heads to minimize stress.

They enjoy making up wild answers to this one. They shove each other and make funny faces ready to make me laugh.

"Maybe they had just been dissed themselves and it showed on their faces," offers Sammy.

Jake shoots his hand straight in the air. "No, they had a bad hair day and their girlfriend laughed at them."

"Maybe they are nearsighted and needed to stare closely to tell who we were?" Rick starts laughing at his own joke.

We all laugh at that.

"So, what do we learn from this?" I lean back.

After some discussion on how easy it is to confuse what we actually see and hear and our interpretations of it, Henry observes, "When we respect others, we can't make snap judgments on what they may think. We don't know and too often we let our own negative energy interpret for us."

George cracks his neck a few times. "I think most of the fights I have with my girlfriend happens because I assume something that doesn't turn out to be true. She was late to our date once and I accused her of all sorts of things. It turns out she had been fired and was talking to her boss. She made me promise that I would ask before I jumped to conclusions. I should have used this exercise."

I sit back against the booth. "Thank you, George. I find it helpful to identify facts or opinions so discussions can stay open. What we often call true changes as we gather more facts."

We enjoy this exercise although it takes mental energy. This filter of tolerance grows as we work at it. It also stops a lot of fights before they get started.

ROB: **Personal Story of a Native Youth Managing for Himself.**

"Here's a tarp - do something so it doesn't flap all over the place on our van." Our youth leader speaks over her shoulder as she strides away.

Amazed that I don't drop the tarp, I look at the bungee cords and figure it out. I start arranging it around the luggage and even order around some other guys to help me.

I was the shy kid who never opened his mouth. How did I get to where I get things done? My first years tore me apart. Dark corners in rooms helped me to stay invisible.

"You a wrong kid. We going to call you 'bad'; that your name from now on," says my Mom when I get into trouble. I like to take things apart, like laptops and guitars. I argue and question everything and everyone, until I start school and then I become a silent loner.

Later, being bullied in school seems like something I deserve. The harder I try to be good, the harsher the bullies. Disaster follows me even when I hide under the teacher's desk or run away from school. They would find me and stuff me in the trash bin.

I've changed a lot from those early years. At eighteen and living on my own, I look back at that stuff that used to happen.

Someone invites me to their grandparent's home in Holbrook, Arizona for a Church youth meeting. I had turned twelve. I don't go to Church. No one in my family goes. I decide to keep my mouth shut and not get too angry at the stuff they might say. To my surprise the kids lead the meeting and we make a video of ourselves about fighting. I look at myself on video and I don't stumble around any worse than the others. Then we reflect. No one lectures or advises me on what I should be doing. No one talks to me about being wrong. I love going to youth group—we do something different every time. For the first time my shoulders don't tighten up when I join in. I belong.

The next big turn-around takes place at the beach in Los Angeles. Seven of us in the Spirit Journey Youth group ride all jumbled up with food and baggage all the way to California. I feel lightheaded when I first see the ocean—someone is actually paying for me to have fun. I join the others in running into the waves and jumping around. Then we bury each other in the sand. I didn't know I could have fun without worrying. The other kids even laugh when I break dance in the water instead of saying "You fool, stop it."

We hike up to the Santa Monica Park above the sandy beach. We hand out bags of sandwiches and stuff we make for those sleeping in the park. We sit down and talk with the homeless who allow us to approach. Placing his hand on his chest a man looks at me straight. "Why you do this? You a saint or something?"

The man sitting next to him sways like he moves with the waves. "You look like you can be somebody. What do you want that's big?" Startled, I look around to see who he means.

He cackles. "You there in your blue striped shirt, what's your dream?" I mumble through something and leave.

Finding a lone tree, I sit by myself a long time in the park just thinking. I think of growing up as a drunk around town like so many of my relatives or maybe hiding in the park under a tree. Sitting on the grass, I reflect on the people I meet now and the mistakes they now admit about themselves. Then I consider all those who push me to go deep. I bounce to my feet and stretch my arms wide.

I am thinking hard about all the hurts I have built up. I have been solitary so much of my life so I figure things out. A lot of stuff I have buried can actually help me make good choices. Stuff like forgiveness loosens up my bitterness. I love being a night owl where I think intensely and not give into others putting me down. When I live through the night to another sun I find myself grinning. I made it again.

Maybe being shy helps me to look inside instead of looking for someone who can rescue me. Whatever—I can now manage hard and easy things. It's in me.

Color Guard, Phoenix, AZ

SECTION THREE
Sacred Paths to Give Meaning

"All things share the same breath-the beast, the tree, the man…the air shares its spirit with all the life it supports."

—Chief Seattle

Acolytes at New Mexico Church

Walking Sacred Paths to Give Meaning

"My little sister just had her first laugh. You have to come to the party." I can hear Danny laughing on the cell phone. I giggle with him at his sheer elation. I know this ceremony is major for the Dine people.

"Who made her laugh? I ask, knowing that person will be paying for the celebration. "How did it happen?"

"My uncle made faces at her until she laughed. We all took turns but he won," he said.

"Who made you laugh first," he asks politely.

I hesitate briefly. "We don't have that custom. I believe that belongs to the Navajo people."

Danny's voice rose. "How could you not have it? I'm sorry. I shouldn't have said that."

"Don't worry about it." I say. "I love going to first laugh parties."

We hang up.

In a few days, I get ready to go to Danny's house. As I arrive, I can smell the mutton cooking on the grill. I walk in and see many of the youth group milling around the house.

Danny talks to the invited people about the ceremony. "In our tradition we know the baby belongs to the world of the holy people and the world of the earth people. At this A'wee Chi'deedloh celebration we believe that the baby laughs to show her joy in joining the earth family. Today we teach my sister Pammy the first steps to a generous life. As each of you pass by her, she will give you rock salt, food, and gifts with the help of my mother and uncle."

We line up to receive our gifts from Pammy's chubby fist, supported by her mother. I taste the salt and receive the plate of mutton and a small gift bag of trade beads.

The youth surround me during the party. Nick asks me, "Do you feel weird at something that is not a Christian tradition?"

Edwin says, "I feel so good being here but I worry about our cultures clashing. What do you think Kaze?"

"All religious traditions have this in common—the practices hold us together not the beliefs," I say. "Natives have power objects, profound stories, chants, and dances. Christians bow the knee, fold their hands in prayer, light candles and say 'Amen.' These practices don't contradict each other. There are many roads to the holy. These roads lead us to love, to generosity and to gratefulness. Sometimes we alternate traditions and sometimes we combine them. Other times we make up our own. As long as we practice those things that open us to a profound path of wholeness, we can explore many faith traditions."

Holy practices involve waking up to the profound in the smallest thing. The following fifteen stories point to four common patterns.

1. Awakening

2. Wonder

3. Compassion

4. Blessing

Awakening

The initial step to a path of wholeness is to pay attention to whatever surrounds us.

"I'm not holy," says Wally. "Everything I do turns out bad for everyone around me.

He just had a fight with his stepdad and was kicked out of his house. We are leaning against the youth van parked outside of his house. My stomach tightens up. I don't know what to say.

"Well," he says. "Why should I care about anything?"

"Sometimes when we are hurt, we close our eyes to stuff around us," I say. "But I see you opening your eyes all the time on our mission trips. I remember when you were the only one who saw the children eating from the dumpster and used your own money to buy them food. Waking up like that to other people is a holy practice."

Wally looks up at me. "I get it. But I'm going to have to work on staying awake."

I laugh. "Me too."

Wonder

Seeing wonder in ordinary things opens us up in extraordinary ways.

One day six of our youth explore the Painted Desert. As we climb over some rocks, we see a broken petrified tree scattered over the landscape. Buddy keeps saying, "Look at that, look at that, look at that." He jumps from log to log chanting this. Buddy laughs as he says, "I just don't have any words. This is so amazing. Would you look at that? That is so awesome. It's just there for anyone to see."

Compassion

Reaching out in compassion enlarges our hearts.

On one of our first trips to Los Angeles, we go to Santa Monica park to hand out brown bags to the homeless who sleep there. "Can't we just put the bag down where they are sleeping?" asks Wayne.

"No, you dog," says Edwin. "We sit down and talk with them. It's respect not charity."

The other kids reassure Wayne that it is easy once you sit down. Wayne shakes his head but goes along with the others.

When they return, Wayne says "I was wrong. The man I talked to worked at making me feel comfortable. He did all the work. I really felt honored that he talked to me. It was awesome."

Blessing

Receiving the blessings of unearned gifts changes us.

One night, five of us drove around Holbrook at night to give blankets to street people. As we approached one group, a Native man thanked us for caring. Tony asked, "We are a Native youth group who is trying to stay out of trouble. Can you pray for us?" The Native immediately started praying for us in Navajo. When he finished, we all got back into the van. Sophie spoke slowly, "That is the most moving prayer I've ever heard and I didn't even understand it. I will never look at a homeless man the same way again."

FIVE PATHS THAT REFLECT AWAKENING

Sacred Path 1: Face Your Pain

Aaron texts the youth group on a social media chat room. "George landed in jail. Since he turned eighteen, he thinks that drinking proves he has become a man. What a stupid rite of passage."

He continues, "Women think having a baby makes them a woman. It's so messed up."

"What do you think makes a man or a woman?" I text back.

"Facing your pain," he replies.

Rafe joins the conversation. "Say more on that Dude. It sounds right but I don't know."

"It helps to have a friend to talk with," Aaron writes. "First, I have to talk to myself and say 'I can do this, I can face it.' It's hard to do that by myself. When Hank came over he told me I looked like s**t. We sat down on the ice cooler and bucket outside. Finally, I could say 'It hurts so much.'"

"I started stuttering. Finally, he says, 'Just say it straight. I've been there.'"

'So I told him the mess I'm in and how bad I am. As I talked I could feel the knot inside my stomach melt away.'"

"I remember the relief I felt when I didn't have to posture about being tough. I made it a part of me and let it go. That's how I face pain."

He stops writing. Natalie sends a smiley face. Everyone says goodbye and signs off.

I sit at my laptop looking into space, feeling both troubled and proud. Arron's insight signals a different path of maturity for the group.

I type up Arron's text and pass it around at our next meeting.

Hank reads out the steps:

- I can face this
- Admit it hurts
- Spell it out without pretense
- Take it into yourself. Breathe deeply as it becomes a part of you
- Let it go
- Move on to the next step

"Any comments on this?" I ask.

"We have spent our whole lives mellowing out when pain appears," admits Edwin. "Pain hurts. When someone puts me down, I feel like a knife has thrust through me. All my satisfaction and happiness drains out through the hole. I want relief immediately. Alcohol and weed do that. But it doesn't last. I can't get enough. And the bitterness is still there. The pain comes back when I have been on a drunk. I guess I need to be reminded to face my pain. You know I got my stepfather's gun once and just held it in my hand. I wanted the pain to end but I couldn't do it."

His best friend Drew sits beside him and hits him on the arm a few times. "You think the rest of us don't know this? Pain spreads around. I don't think we can even do the first step of saying we can face pain, unless we have some kind of ceremony, like when we sit in a circle and pass the Eagle feather around or we burn sage."

"You know what else helps?" Hank asks. "Remember when we received the Eucharist for the first time at our baptism. We learned that the bread is broken just like us and we can take the broken part inside us and eat it. We don't have to pretend that everything is okay. We make it a part of us and we are a part of the Creator. I feel like I do when I greet the sun and breathe in Mother Earth and make it a part of me. Maybe our pain has to do with our not feeling a part of something bigger. I think we either face our pain or have the pain be our face."

Natalie says, "I like this list but the first step is the hardest. I have to have hope before I believe that I can face pain. How do you get hope?"

Hank says, "This is something we just have to jump in and do. When we face pain once, it gets easier. That's why it is a path. It opens up a direction. Hope grows out of it."

I stay silent. They know how to help each other on their journey.

Sacred Path 2: Inventing Identity

"That's ghetto," says Rob pointing to a car with four flat tires near the city park in Winslow.

"Yeah," replies Timmy. "And it sure is rez."

Rob shifts from one foot to the other. "I wish that being Native didn't always mean being ghetto or rez."

We stand around our white van staring at the mostly empty street. Litter swirls around the dilapidated mobile homes. Drew clears his throat. "I'm torn between what I mainly think about myself and what I sort of believe I have become. I don't want to be tied down to being ghetto but I want to learn from our old ways at the same time."

Timmy lifts his head. "Remember that exercise we do about how we see ourselves? Choose a symbol that is about you; maybe one that is not complete but in the right direction."

"I remember," says Rob. "We placed about sixty animals, plant and human figures on the table. Each one of us chose one item that had our qualities. We didn't tell anyone the quality we chose. Then everyone else had to say how we had some quality of that figure. I took a wild horse because it had so much energy. I remember being told that I could go where I wanted, that I move fast and that girls thought I was sexy. After everyone stopped laughing I told them that 'energy' was the quality I most treasured. I was impressed by what they saw in me."

Drew says. "I would choose differently now. I would choose a river rock instead of an action figure. I remember when the priest in Los Angeles gave us all a polished stone to symbolize our decision to work with street people. So much in my life has been rough or ugly. I like thinking of a stone that has been tumbled over and over by a river until it turns smooth and beautiful with all the colors showing."

We end the discussion with an agreement to hold another symbol workshop soon.

The following week, we try a different type of identity workshop. We discuss what is important to us and write on a post-it. Then they choose an artistic medium to express it.

Zach, who plans to enlist in the military on his eighteenth birthday, creates a clay figure. He molds a muscular young man bent over with pain and holding a globe. When he finishes, he reworks the globe so that it begins to fragment. He talks about it quietly. "I'm joining the Marines because I can't stand being the oldest son anymore and not being able to keep my family from coming apart. I can't stop the drinking or the abuse of my siblings. I can't do anything but leave."

He moves around the table picking up one thing after the other. Finally, he takes some more clay and makes himself a gun in place of the world. Our eyes fix on him but no one says anything. Then he takes away the gun. He creates a medicine pouch and puts that into his hand with his other hand sprinkling corn pollen. "I don't know what I think. I can't stand by and do nothing and I can't kill people. I want to be one who blesses the land. That is something I can do." His body stills and he collapses into a chair.

Still none of us speak. We don't have to. He has done the difficult work of finding what works for him.

Sacred Path 3: Going Deep

Sometimes I lay awake at night wondering if the youth have learned anything. I worry if they can stay alive until they reach eighteen. I fear that their pain gets covered over with a superficial scab instead of real healing.

One night as I adjust my pillow, shots ring out and the sirens begin wailing. I hate these sounds. I imagine one of my youth lying dead on the street or in an ambulance. I stay awake, waiting for a phone call, then get up and read to calm my mind.

The next day I decide to visit some homes to see if a disaster happened in Holbrook while I slept. I berate myself at my unending anxiety.

Hank answers my knock. "Did anything happen last night? I heard the sirens," I ask.

Hank pats me on the shoulder. "Slow down. We would call you if anything happened. We watch out for each other. We are a family now."

I feel comforted. After ten years with the youth group, we grow deeper each year.

"How did we get to be such a caring group of people?" I ask.

Hank grins. Have the other groups been different? How many youth groups have we had?"

I run my hand through my hair as I answer. "We always have some change-over when kids turn eighteen. We just mix in the new with the older group. We probably are on our third complete turnover."

"Have we always done the same things?" Hank asks.

"We tried different things but we usually do some kind of serious stuff, something fun and something compassionate. The key to what binds and keeps us thoughtful, however, revolves around our reflections." I say. "That's what keeps us caring."

I remember Marty saying when we returned from Los Angeles, "If we didn't ask our reflective questions over and over, I would not remember what to say when we return from a trip. I know that when my mom asks me what I did at school, I always say 'Nothing much. I never remember the details.'"

"Why don't you let me do the reflection at the next meeting?" Hank asks. "I like knowing a new skill." I quickly agree.

We set up a meeting with a few of the older youth to learn the reflection questions. We sit around a table at the youth center in front of a chalk board. I write the questions on the board as I talk it through.

"If we don't reflect on an experience, it disappears from our memory. To reduce this memory loss, we typically ask four simple questions at the end of an experience. "What do you remember? What were your ups and downs? What do you learn from it?" And sometimes we add "How are you different because of it? In short, we begin by keeping it factual, ponder our emotional overlays and pinpoint where it means something and how we change."

"Why do we do this?" Drew asks?

I sit back in my chair. "When we first began, everyone would jump to the meaning without remembering exactly what we did. I loved seeing someone like Buddy throwing back his head laughing saying, 'I had fun the whole day.' But then he didn't remember what he did by evening.

By pointing to specific activities, like hiking up the mountain, we paint a composite picture of a full day and not just the left over emotion."

Arron asks, "Can we ask different questions?"

"Of course," I say. "It seems most effective to go through different levels of questions. Everyone can easily answer the first objective level. "What are the different things we did today, both horrible or happy? It puts us all on the same page.

The second level involves emotions. 'Where were you up? Down?' Almost everyone likes to answer these. Sherry usually says 'Breakfast wins my down. It tasted like cardboard.' Zach told us 'My down was when we saw someone drunk on the street and laughed at him.'"

Danny says, "I never liked to answer the 'down question.' I felt I was being disloyal to our group. And I always had more than one 'up' to share."

"I think the third level has the most importance. Talking about what we learned helps us to see the impact," says Arron.

Drew blurted out "I learned that I can be thankful for what I have and stop whining about the little things I don't have."

"Now we come to the last level of questions." I say. "We don't expect many answers to this. As long as we hear the question, it makes us think. Usually we ask 'How are you different because of what you saw or did?'"

"Thanks for saying we don't have to answer it. I find it difficult," says Drew. "How does this get answered usually?"

Danny responds, "Lisa gave a great answer last summer. She said 'I look at the people on the street and I know that I have more choices than they do. I don't want to lie to myself anymore about what I have to put up with.'"

We then practiced the method several times among ourselves until we felt comfortable.

Several years after my retirement, Jose calls to talk about a meeting they had with some of the younger kids. "I led with the questions you taught us. One of the youth stole a Gameboy from a young boy and hid it in his backpack. We started with a sacred circle and a sage blessing. We put the Eagle feather in a chair in the middle. Our first question detailed what happened. We had to get through some posturing and lies. We talked about the hurt of a friend stealing from us and we talked about the betrayal, anger and hurt. The Gameboy was returned with a quick man hug and apology. It was hard then to get responses for the third question. Tina said, 'I think that I have to keep remembering that we can start over again.' Timmy volunteered to answer the last question of how he might change. 'I usually just dismiss a theft or mess-up and hope that it goes away by itself. I realize that I can actually do something to help.' With that we became a solid group, ready to move forward. The questions really help even though the answers don't always seem so smart."

Our ability to reflect on something keeps stuff from festering and cements the event in our memory. The reflection somehow reframes the event into a story worth remembering and a path to follow.

Sacred Path 4: Listen with Respect

"I want each of you to say one thing during the discussion." I turn to face all the kids. "We need to have our voices heard if we want the Native American youth program to be supported."

We sit in a congregational meeting on outreach programs in Colorado. They give donations to youth groups who impress them. However, our young people remain silent. The meeting does not go well.

We retreat to the Church kitchen table chatting. Every pantry item in sight gets picked up or displaced several times.

I toss a potato masher from hand to hand, gathering my thoughts. I assume they stayed silent because they have been taught from a young age that speaking before the elder speaks is disrespectful.

"I know this violates your tradition but you have something important to contribute."

Sophie tosses her hair out of her eyes. "They won't let us talk. They seem so interested in what they have to say that they never pause." She leans over the sink examining the drain.

"And they interrupt us if we hesitate," says Ken. "They don't care what we have to say."

We talk about listening. And what it means in their tradition.

Marty shoves his hands deep into his pockets, making his jeans sag even more. "My grandmother taught me that Elders have earned respect and deserve our listening. We listen to learn. As you age, you remember the importance of things, especially for the tribe. She told me that I should practice talking with the other youth so I would know if my words serve the tribe. Sometimes I don't remember this but mostly I try to practice respect."

Elliot, a congregational member, walks in and looks around the group. "I wish you kids talked more. We want to hear what you think."

Most look away or down at the floor.

Since I am an elder, I speak up. "We get the feeling from your group that people are waiting for us to shut up so they can tell us what they think. Few people listen respectfully. They have a pocketful of responses regardless of what we have said. Then they pounce on us for not talking when we don't get a chance. What do you think happened in there?"

Although taken aback by my not so tactful words, he considers it. "You may have a point. Your kids seem to take their time in responding which could mean they take it seriously. We are used to saying whatever just comes out of our mouths."

I carefully explain the tradition of respectfully listening first to what the older people have to say.

Ken stands up to speak to the man, "It's okay. We get that a lot. We have two different traditions that don't fit together in conversations. We are taught to *listen to respect*, not to *listen to respond*. After someone talks we maintain a silence to think about what is said rather than just talk."

Elliot lowers his head. He shakes the hand of each youth and apologizes for not "listening to respect."

Later in the van, we talk about what we learn from this conversation.

"We have to ask people to let us talk without interruption and maybe have a moderator point to who speaks next," says Marty. "I wish I could say that I listen to them respectfully but I don't. Resentment fills my ears. If I want to honor my tradition I have to make an effort to *listen to respect* to everyone."

"How do we do that?" I ask.

Sherry says. "Maybe we can burn the sage before we go to a meeting and remind ourselves to listen to everyone.

Ken's eyes light up. "We can each tell about one thing we remember, like we do after sermons."

"I know," says Buddy. "When we speak, we repeat what the last person says so they know we haven't changed the subject and are responding to them."

This becomes a turning point for the group. In later meetings with different cultures, the youth practice this skill of respect. I feel myself dancing each time I listen to these young people working hard to enrich relationships with another culture. Waking up to our heritage in how to listen becomes a holy path to authentic dialogue.

Sacred Path 5: Doing the Unexpected

Stamping his feet, Zach glares at me, "Why are we doing this? Why can't we go to the amusement park in Flagstaff like we did before? We had fun there."

We sit under a tree at our local park as we plan our next big trip.

Drew looks at Zach. "Chill, Dude. We don't learn anything until we get out of our comfort zone. Our brain loosens up when we do something different."

Zach says, "We've been to Skid Road before. That's not new."

Drew responds, "He's right. If we go, we need to do something different. Last time in Los Angeles, we sat down in the park and ate with the homeless. What's our next step?"

"Instead of an hour, let's spend all day really getting to know the people. You know they talk to us because we have dark skin. They see us as one of them, especially the way we dress," says Ken.

The youth solidify their plan to gather nice shirts, socks, and food in a backpack to hand out. Everyone takes two backpacks apiece.

We arrive at one of the streets in Skid Road. Trash fills the gutters. Men and women wander the streets with sacks and sometimes sleeping bags on their back or in a grocery cart. No one looks at us. I park the van and sit on a bench under a tree. People glance at us and then go back sitting on the bench looking down at the ground.

Rafe says, "You will be with us, right?"

"No, I can no longer walk long distances. I will sit on the bench under the tree with the street people here."

Some faces flush. "Are we going alone?"

"Yes," I say. "You know what to do. Just spend the day talking with people you meet. Make some friends."

Danny shrugs. "Come on. We planned this. We said we'd go off by ourselves and spend the day listening and showing people we notice them."

"Yeah," says Zach. "But I didn't think we would actually do it."

The kids look at each other but say "Okay, let's do it."

They form two teams and I say goodbye bravely, like sending my own kids to their first day of school. As they begin to walk the very dirty streets of Skid Road, Rick and George turn to me to ask, "What if they attack us for food? Do we run?"

"Just talk to them," I suggest.

They all have extra money to invite street people to eat lunch with them after they give away the backpacks. They walk away without a backward glance. I sit on a bench that circles a tree and begin talking to those around me. Having white hair gives me an aura of not being dangerous. They question me about being there but soon we have an interesting conversation on sleeping spaces in the city.

When the youth return around 4 p.m., they discuss the different encounters. George talks rapidly, "You should have seen the men in the wheelchairs on one corner. They kept saying 'Thank you' for the backpacks. They were so happy to talk with us."

Rafe says, "We talked to a naked man who danced on the street. He loved his new backpack so he gave us a special dance. It was so cool."

I ask, "Did he seem mentally unstable?"

To my surprise, Rafe offers other alternatives. "He may have been angry. Someone may have stolen all his clothes. He could just be tired of no one paying attention to him. He talks like everyone else."

I had thought that the impact of the day would be seeing the plight of the homeless. Instead, they talked about their ease being among people who used to seem different

"I expected to look down on the people I met, to judge them harshly," says Rafe. "I didn't anticipate finding people who act with different motives just like I do. I didn't expect to become close to people like I do with my own brothers. I surprised myself to discover friends."

Throughout the week in California, the youth kept referring to the people by name. They never seem to run out of things that happened on our day in Skid Road.

Doing something new woke us up to another way to care without judgement.

THREE PATHS THAT REFLECT WONDER

Sacred Path 6: Greeting the Sun

Some of the young people give a sage blessing at the Episcopal Church of St. John's La Verne, California. During the service, we notice the families taking big breaths as they smell the pungency of sage. We then pack our van to return to Northern Arizona. It is stuffed with unclaimed smelly socks and tee-shirts along with other mementos from our mission trip.

John and Michael, two mentors from the church took us on a yearly hike to gather white sage. Although we stuff it into a black trash bag thrown in the back, the smell permeates the van during our trip home. While we stand outside the van to say goodbye, one of the older youth takes a deep breath. "I feel like we are floating home in a temple fueled by sage and not gas."

After members of the congregation thank the kids for their week of service and the Native blessing on Sunday, one woman asks how often we use the sage.

"Not often," Rob says. "Except, of course, when we greet the sun. You know, we give thanks for each new day and our life."

Stupefied, the woman asks, "How often do you do that?"

Surprised, Rob looks to see if it is a joke. "The sun comes up every day. My grandmother did it until she died. Now my mother wakes us each morning. When I move into my own apartment, I will be doing it. I always have my corn pollen and sage."

The lady says, "You give thanks every day?"

"Of course," he says. "My grandfather used to stand outside the window and throw water on us if we stayed in bed. How do you start your day?"

"I should be thankful but I never seem to have the time," the lady says.

We talk about this driving home. "I thought Christians prayed," says Chuck.

"They may not have the spiritual discipline for prayer on a daily basis," I say. "Not everyone knows about your spirituality. How long have you been doing this ceremony?"

"All my life," says Edwin. "But my stepfather isn't Native and he makes fun of it so we do it when he is not around."

Other comments emerge on the difficulty of scattering the corn pollen and lighting the sage in an urban setting. They punch each other as one says, "I open my front door and scatter pollen on the sidewalk and think to myself, that ain't right. People will step on it." Yet the youth still take time for the ritual words and actions.

Rob assures me, "You know, just having the sage in the van makes me proud that I am native and I know sacred things. I can smell my grandfather's hogan with cedar logs soaked in years of blessings."

Zach looks out the window and whispers, "I remember when we first started using sage and Native blessings. At first I didn't know how they fit in a Christian youth group. Somehow we weave it together until I only see and smell the same goodness."

I don't know what else to say. These prayers of thanksgiving focus our day declaring there is goodness in this day, regardless of the lack of food or housing. They keep us on our path. Instead of writing off a bad day as useless, we practice noticing the wondrous.

At the beginning of a mission trip, Hank blessed the van and us with the Eagle feather and sage. We stood in a bleak parking lot surrounded by empty cars. A drunken Native man across the street saw us; he ran over to join our sacred circle. The kids moved to give him space to enter. Slowly, Hank holding the eagle feather moved to each person directing the smoke of the sage. The stranger stood up straight and motioned the smoke toward himself. When we finished, he thanked us over and over for letting him participate. Drunk or sober, he knew how to receive the blessing with both hands.

Sacred Path 7: Celebration Ceremonies

Too many transitions and achievements go ignored in families who barely hold together through frequent crises. Early in our time as a group we began to hold celebrations to notice milestones.

Over the years we try different spiritual practices of celebration. Once when the kids fool around while other natives stand at attention during an honor song, I turn to face them with my meanest face and hiss "Stop it." After the ceremony Aaron wrinkles his forehead. "Still angry?"

"Yes." I bite my lip to stop the anger spilling out. "And I will remain angry until we talk this through."

We find a place to sit in a circle and talk about what happened. We raise all sorts of issues including them not honoring their own tradition and not liking my public rebuke. I finally admit my anger, "I stand responsible for you and I feel shamed that you were disrespectful in the ceremony. I forgot that your behavior reflects on you, not me."

I continue, "I don't know if I am sorry or not that I told you to stop."

Arron says, "Can we talk among ourselves for a few moments?"

I agree and leave the circle.

When they ask me to return, they all sit up straight in the circle and look at the center. Aaron says, "We apologize. We were wrong. We were disrespectful to the drummers and we knew it. We know how to behave at an honor song. We want to be in balance again. We also ask that when you are angry that you whisper to one person who can whisper to us. And we want some of us to be the ones who point out when we mess up and not just you."

I agree and we move to a new level of awareness. Someone stands up and removes his ball cap. "We need something to bring beauty back into our walk, we are too sad. We've been through too much to just leave this."

We finally pull out one of the ceremonies we use and chant it together:

Honor the Sacred. Honor the Earth. Honor our Mother. Honor the Elders.

Honor all with whom we share the Earth: Four leggeds, two leggeds, winged ones, swimmers, crawlers, plant and rock people. Walk in Balance And Beauty

Then we go out and eat ice cream to celebrate our reconciliation.

Since that time we are careful to not let things fester and to end with a celebration of our kinship with each other and all creation.

Together we learn many ways to celebrate. We add ceremonies and words that touch us and bring us closer to honor our collective journey. We may bake a cake, burn sage, chant, exchange gifts, or sprinkle sanctified water.

On occasion, we hold a ceremony for those who walk in the Spirit world. This stamps the lives of those who have gone as loved and missed. "I didn't know that I could still cry about it" says Rolland who grieves for a friend who killed himself. These celebrations pay tribute to the importance of every life.

We often mix traditional native ceremonies with historical Christian rites. Our celebrations bind us as a community.

During one of our baptisms we arrange the cross, the sage, and the turquoise necklace on the altar. Bishop Michael Vono blesses them before they are presented to the youth being baptized. After the ceremony, Glen carefully stores these items in a wooden box. "These are not just stuff. They have been blessed. I'm not sure how but that means something."

Tears and laughter well up when we use holy practices to mark significances. To commemorate birth, death and the interval in-between requires an openness to something awesome. We heal and grow when we celebrate that which is radically important.

Sacred Path 8: Creating Stories

Timmy comes running out of the church's community hall. "I hate it. I won't go back in."

Panicking, I ask "Did someone hurt you?"

"No," he says, with his face twisted and his body held tight. "They get in my face and ask me a million questions, like the police or the principal."

I sit with him. The youth mill around among the empty tables, and running their hands over every available space, waiting for my response.

In Native culture, talking about yourself counts as an aggressive act because calling attention to yourself amounts to bragging. They are uncomfortable with inquisitive questions.

"Why do they want to know everything about us?" Nick asks. "I feel like a freak who has no privacy."

We talk until we finally figure out the cultural disconnect. Anglo society asks questions to find out about an individual. Native society tells stories that place the individual in a community. For Natives, personal questions rather than stories reduce them to being an orphan without relationships.

Betty tells us about the last Native dance she attended. "If we don't know each other, we exchange our mother and father's clan names. Then we talk about what goes on around us, like the food and dances. We don't parade our past around."

"Tell me what that story tells us about Natives?" I ask.

"Who we are related to is the most important thing," Nick says. "We don't need to tell people about what we do."

From that conversation, we decided to educate congregations on how to talk with Native youth.

Now when we visit Churches, we suggest that adults talk about themselves first and then pick a related topic and say "Tell me about it or tell me something about yourself." This puts it into story form and the youth can talk about their identity or not.

Our best conversations bind us together and carry us to the profound.

"What did your grandmother tell you about this?" has become the most fruitful question I can ask. Everyone can answer. In the Native traditions, the grandmother usually carries the title of storyteller.

Danny shares one story, "My grandmother told me that when

children were taken away by force, bitterness took root in the heart and tears never dried up. The way she described it, I could feel the pain of my family. I became scared that it would happen again. I get scared every time the police come by our house. But then my grandmother told me how they listened to the wind, hearing their ancestors speak. Then they were able to hold their heads high. She gave me details on how they got through it. I will never forget her stories and how proud they make me. I will tell stories the same way to my future kids."

Wally, grieving for his deceased grandmother, says, "She told me not to use drink or drugs to take away the pain. Remember the pain of our people when the soldiers forced us to move away from our land with no food or clothing. So many people died and yet we sang on the way; we helped each other; and we kept our stories. We didn't get drunk. I still feel her presence in the spirit world."

"This story moves me," I say. "It connects us to the long line of ancestors who shape us. When we just relay facts, the threads fragment that connect us to our history. I've heard you all talk about painful episodes of being hit or neglected. These isolated incidents leave you bereft. When you can tie these experiences into your story of your relationships and your dignity, they can heal."

Stories are about sharing, not imposing. Being story tellers encourages us to shape our journey to find meaning.

THREE PATHS THAT REFLECT COMPASSION

Sacred Path 9: Encouraging

Fifteen of the youth sign up for our youth leadership team. We meet in a small enclosed room at the back of the Church. Rafe pushes his question out rapidly. "How do we make the younger kids do what we want?"

I sigh at this desire for control. "We don't. We encourage them."

Rafe explodes with a belligerent sputter. "How are we supposed to do that?"

I hand out Post-its. "Everyone write down three qualities you want the younger kids to have."

Each picks their top written item. We go around the table listing them. "I want them to be responsible and pick up after themselves." "I want them to speak up for themselves." "I want them to have their own opinions." "I want them to tolerate those who are different." "I want them to be kind." "I want them to be respectful to people and to the stuff we have."

"Okay," I say, "Whenever any of the younger kids show the quality you pick, you tell him or her something that is encouraging, like 'cool,' or 'way to go' or give a thumbs up. If someone gives their own opinion, you compliment him or her immediately. The youth will see what you value and will begin to do that more. Telling kids what you value goes over their heads. When you compliment something they do, they get the value."

Jake immediately jams his baseball cap on backward. "This won't work."

George yawns. "Let's try it."

We practice some verbal and non-verbal affirmations.

As we pour out our small collection of different ways to say "cool," we burst into laughter when someone offers "Gold Star" as a viable accolade.

"How do you say 'good job' with gestures?" I ask next.

"We can pat them on the shoulder." "We can do a high five or thumbs up." "Maybe, we use just a smile and a nod for the girls."

I instruct them. "Nonverbal gestures help to bypass someone's embarrassment about a compliment. Kids will respond quicker to thumbs up than a verbal compliment. If you say anything, make sure you don't look at them and make it short like 'awesome,'"

I send them off to circulate around the room where the younger kids are playing pool or on the computers.

Soon I hear exclamations all over the room, "That's tight." "Good for you." "Cool, Dude." "Keep it up."

At the end of the day, the energy level is high.

Drew reports, "I complimented Danny and he started smiling at everyone."

"Calvin offered his computer to someone waiting so I punched him lightly on the shoulder and said 'Good for you.' He just beamed."

"I can't believe how much happier they seem today." "Compliments really change them." "This may actually work." "Can we have more than one quality we can encourage?"

A cheerfulness spreads through me. "When you focus on one quality at a time rather than cheering about everything, then the one thing becomes special. Also you want to encourage them to grow in their journey and that takes focus and time. We can add a new quality every three days. It takes time for a quality to be integrated."

Learning to encourage rather than give orders becomes the window to compassion.

Sacred Path 10: Paying Attention

We park the van near rows of people sleeping on the streets of Skid Road. Most do not register our presence. As we get out, Hank speaks quietly to our group. "Head toward those who seem withdrawn. Greet them and if they don't want to talk, move on. Otherwise, say something about yourself and ask how things are here, like the weather and the food places. Keep it low key. They don't expect anyone to notice them and they may be fearful."

He frowns. "Oh, don't wake up anyone."

A long exhale from the group with a quiet "Duh."

I wait around the van for their return. Soon I see a cluster of teens bouncing on their toes surrounded by street people drifting in and out of their orbit. They wave goodbye and get into the van.

We drive to a park so Drew can lead the reflection. The kids sprawl on the grass and their eyes soften.

Drew breathes out slowly. "How many invisible people did you talk with?"

"One man in a faded blue shirt looked around when I spoke to him," says Norm. "He thought I mistook him for someone else. He looked so pleased when I stayed to talk."

Calvin wrings his hands. "The first guy I saw looked like he wanted to hit me and I stepped back. I put the food sack on the ground and stepped away. He picks it up and starts eating. Finally, he says thanks. He gives me a little smile and walks backwards until he turns a corner."

"Name some awesome experiences or a difficult time?" Drew continues.

Pulling out blades of grass one at a time, George speaks, "The man I spoke to kept yelling at me to tell him who sent me. He never stopped shouting. I began to wonder why I did speak to him."

Jimmy says, "A little girl runs toward me when she sees the food. She stops and waits. I immediately hand her the sack of food. She thanks me and runs to her mother showing her the chips inside. They laughed and hugged. I felt so good."

Drew asks the third level of questions. "What did you learn today?"

Different youth respond. "The strangest looking people can be interesting." "People can be happy even when they live on the streets." "Not everyone thinks that good things can happen to them."

Drew finally asks "How are you different?"

"I used to be more shy," says Betty. "Now, I feel I can go new places and do many more things."

Zach jerks his head up. "I enjoy paying attention to the ignored people. It's funny. I didn't think I would. It's like seeing turquoise in a hidden dirt pile."

Paying attention has become a simple path; a holy practice that involves time, compassion and the willingness to put ourselves out for others.

Sacred Path 11: Prayer Lens

Blood flows everywhere in the house. Marty has been in a street fight and a knife sliced his side. After the ambulance takes him to the Winslow hospital his father and cousin clean up the blood on the floor and furniture. His brother Wally calls me from Phoenix and begs me to pray for his brother. I drive to the hospital praying incoherently. My mind couldn't focus. I kept muttering "Have mercy." I couldn't think of other words.

As I sat at Marty's bedside, other youth arrived at the hospital.

"I don't know what to pray for," I confess. "Prayer endures as such a sticky word. Different faiths have different meanings." I stop to think things through. The youth keep staring at me. "Every religion includes prayer for discerning the sacred, for being open to forces of goodness. I don't know why I have such difficulty with it."

Aaron says, "That doesn't tell us how to pray. Most of my school friends don't even use the word 'prayer.' They talk about sending good vibes instead of prayers. Why do we pray?"

"Prayer concentrates and focuses the holiness we see around us. It lets up lift up concerns even if we don't know to whom or to what form we pray," I say.

We spent the rest of the night sitting by Marty's bed talking about our concerns and issues.

When I drove home that next morning, I thought of the time when we began as a youth group. I prayed out loud, feeling like a hypocrite as I stumbled through words that didn't seem to fit either what I believed or what they understood. Since then, we've spent a lot of time creating a new frame of reference for old rites and words. It never became easy.

One day as the group hiked up a hill I hear Sammy talking behind me. "It seems so clear that God has to be bigger than anything we can define."

I stop to breathe deeply. "We need different ways to stand before the sacred. A god up there or a god that stands apart from us does not hack it."

He mutters "Yeah."

When we reach the top of the hill, we sit on the ground. I turn to the youth. "Over the years we have changed our images about the Holy. Do you remember when we wrote, drew and photographed prayers rather than just saying them?"

"That was fun," said Rolland. We took our cameras and took pictures of things we found awesome."

Nancy says, "We also drew pictures of people we wanted to pray for. You told us that we never know what will be awesome for us."

Sophie says, "That feels so good to me. I do get pulled into awesome times, like when I am given a second chance at school or I see a sunset."

"When and why do you pray?" I ask. "How is it connected to your faith?"

"For me, my faith tells me that I can start over again. I mess up bad sometimes. No matter how many times I mess up, I get more than a second or a third or a fourth chance. My chances go on forever." Henry wipes his forehead and eyes and stares at his hands.

Chuck says, "It helps to know that I belong, that I am a part of history and that I will never be an outcast again. I pray that I may never be forgotten."

Natalie says, "Is it selfish to only pray for ourselves?"

"There are all sorts of prayers," I say. "You need compassion for yourself as much as for other people or issues." Natalie nods with tears in her eyes.

"Sometimes," says Rolland, "I feel a world opens itself in front of me and invites me in. It is when my heart fills with thanks or when I see something truly awesome, like the smile on the face of a street person. I can't explain it but it's like God is around."

Danny says, "When I pray it is like something being poured into me that I then pour out; like I am a big fire hose of water except it is energy that is being poured in and out. I am claimed by goodness, not failure or prison or hatred."

"I pray without words," says Rick. "I burn the sage or sit in the wind watching birds and I become thankful. I don't say 'thank you.' I just sit in it."

This becomes our lens of faith—to step beyond words and give shape to that which cannot be contained. We uncover words and metaphors that give a shape to our belief without trying to entrap our understanding of God in a box.

Our prayers allow us to draw forth whatever keeps us going forward in beauty.

I offer one of the prayers the Native youth wrote.

"Give thanks for all four legged, two legged, winged ones, swimmers, crawlers, and plant and rock people; for all growing things and all that makes up the earth and seas.

We live in respect that we may be proud to be your people."

FOUR PATHS THAT REFLECT BLESSING

Sacred Path 12: Marking Holy Ground

We put on our hairnets and plastic gloves to serve in the soup kitchen in Skid Row, Los Angeles. The lines fill quickly with people who shuffle, grunt, flinch, shrug, or sag. Some thank us, some avert their faces and some challenge us. We stand behind the counter handing out food with a cheerful greeting.

Jake says "I don't know why I feel so good about this. I thought it would be boring to spend hours handing out food."

"Every time we come here, something happens to us." I reply. "We get rid of old pictures that divide us from people who are different. Somehow, we find ourselves blessed."

"I know what you mean," says Jake. "I feel like I get compassion just by handing out bread."

On this morning, our youth group once again distributes a hot meal and drinks in the Midnight Mission in the center of Skid Row. Each of us hands out one item of food for hours to over 700 people. Facing street people who submit to the indignity of handouts has us blinking back tears.

Sharon wipes the sweat out of her eyes as we rest after the breakfast line closes down. "It takes effort to greet each person with a "What up?" or "How's your day? I got so tired of saying 'Do you want some eggs?' No matter how many rebuffs we got, we hung in there even though some sounded hostile."

"One tall guy keeps picking out the ham in his scrambled eggs and throwing it on the floor. He glares at me and tells me he is Muslim," says Edwin. "I wanted to say that I didn't make the eggs but it didn't seem appropriate. I believe that he wanted to be angry. I felt so bad that I didn't have the right food for him."

Glen says "No matter how many people come through the line, I still want one more to be there. It's like the whole line is located on Holy Ground."

"What do you mean?" asks Buddy. "That sounds pious."

"Naw, it's stuff we already do. You know how we sprinkle pollen on the ground at a ceremony to declare it sacred ground? I wish we could do that or light sage so they could keep their heads up," he says.

Glen adds, "It's like the Great Spirit flies around the room like an eagle shielding them but they can't see it. They only see the food in front of them."

Before we leave, we gather in the kitchen and pour some corn pollen in the four sacred directions. We straighten our shoulders as we walk toward the street.

Back at the L.A. Church where we sleep in a back room, we sprawl on the floor. We can't stop talking about the soup kitchen.

Buddy throws his head back. "When we first started talking about Holy Ground, I faked it. I pretended I understood. I have been in a lot of traditional ceremonies so I should know. Then it happened. I shared my sandwich with one of the street people and we sat there chewing on turkey and cheese just hanging. I felt like a carrier for something good. I swear the ground started getting hot and I want to take off my shoes. I know our feet stands on holy dirt. I wish I had my prayer bundle or could say a chant that scores it. Does that sound crazy?"

"No," I respond. "Sometimes when I have felt diminished and without hope, something I didn't plan happens. Maybe a stranger smiles at me or the rain smells so pungent. The brain fog dissipates and I notice things intensely. At that moment, everything shows up as significant. I can't explain it. I only know the holy is present, like a respectful atmosphere."

A mutter of "Yeah, that's it," fills the room.

Marking the earth and seeing certain times as sacred become the signposts in our journey, revered as turning points in our growing.

Sacred Path 13: Creating Sacred Space

Drawing his arms close to his body, Jimmy, a Hopi youth, tells us his nation puts prayer sticks at special shrines on their land. A tourist had stolen some and it stunned him.

"We make a Pahos with special feathers and bury it in the ground which has a sacred significance, usually near water or a cave. It is our prayer on Hopi sacred ground. Why would anyone steal our prayers?"

We are so drained by his sadness that the air seems to suffocate us. Words fall heavy as we sit around the table at the youth center.

Jimmy twisted his baseball cap in his hands. "I hate it when others make fun of the places we hold as sacred. How would they like it if we desecrated an altar or a cemetery? It makes me so mad."

Norm paces up and down the room. "I don't live on the rez. I feel cut off from our sacred places. We mark places on our mission trips as holy. Why can't we do that closer to home?"

"You can create a sanctuary in your home," I say.

"How do we do that?" asks Jimmy.

"You designate a space in your home where you place items that have sacred significance for you. What would that be for you?" I ask.

Hank fidgets by rearranging the décor items on the table. "I have a box of traditional sanctified objects. My uncle left me his eagle feather and I have rocks from the four sacred mountains. I keep it under my bed now. That doesn't seem right."

We brainstorm objects that hold meaning and where to place them. Some suggest hanging them on the wall. Others can make space on their desk, chair or a private place outside.

Norm starts chuckling, "I can put it on the roof. No one goes up there. I can cut out a piece of tarp to put over it."

This becomes a week's project. "It has to have water," they insist. So they either find a shell or container for water. They locate feathers that signify Father Sky. They arrange dirt or rocks for Mother Earth. They share the details at our next meeting.

Some of the youth have a picture of their family, a broken shell from the ocean, a medicine bag, a pouch of corn pollen, rocks from the four directions, sage, cedar bundles, a cross, the Book of Common Prayer—anything that reminds them of their defining moments.

Hank closes his eyes as he recounts creating a holy space in his shared bedroom. "I have my cross hanging up on a nail. Then my abalone shell with sage to burn within it goes on my chair near my bed. I also have my box with an eagle feather under my bed. When I sit on my bed I feel enclosed by things which have a spirit in themselves. I want a part of my home to keep the holy in my face so when the yelling starts I can keep balanced."

"You should see my roof," says Norm. "My uncle asks me why I kept taking stuff up there. I just laugh. I cut out a piece of tarp and stapled three sides to the roof. One side stays open to hide the objects. I place a plastic bag full of sage on a kitchen mat, holding it down with rocks from the four sacred mountains. Another plastic bag holds my corn pollen. I love to sit there and smell the sage burning. It completes me."

Rob folds his hands in his lap. "When I pray in my room, I go to a deep place in the center of my body. When I return, I look at those things that remind me that holiness surrounds me in things I see every day. I breathe better."

We look at Jimmy who started us thinking about the desecration of Native holy places. He says, "This helps. I worry too much about living in the city. Being able to choose places where we can smell the holy turns me around."

Sacred Path 14: Return to Wholeness

"When I spent three months in Juvenile Detention, I changed several times," Rolland says with a radiant smile. "My anger filled me up for the first two weeks. Then I became resigned to doing nothing. As you visited me every week, I began to hope that I would get back to normal and nothing would change. In my last month I finally started to think about who I wanted to be. By that time my posturing about being a scrappy fighter and a cool dude disappeared. I felt incomplete and wrong somehow. I still work on it. I want to be complete and that means not doing stupid things to put me back in jail."

The youth in the room stare down at their feet or look away. No one says anything. Finally, he finishes, "I want to like myself and have a future."

"For the rest of you, when do you feel whole and complete?" I ask. We sit in comfortable chairs more or less in a circle in the community center. Some kids have moved their chairs to look in different directions.

Rick places his arms on the chair back. "It was my birthday celebration. When the priest blessed me with the sign of the cross on my forehead, I felt like my past was not going to hold me back. I felt like a new person."

Zach shifts in his chair. "Once I sat on my roof trying to get my anger to go away when I saw clouds drifting towards me. I kept waiting for the clouds to reach me. I couldn't leave until the clouds appeared overhead. Then it came to me. I don't want a stupid sign. I want to be a different person, not filled with all this stuff. And like that, I felt cleared up with something like hope or happiness. I didn't even notice if the clouds had moved over me or not. I didn't want to do anything, just be glad about being there."

"For me, when I sprinkle corn pollen and thank the Creator for a new day, I feel like I don't have to do anything more. Everything is in place the way it should be," says Henry playing with his napkin.

"I like to kneel," George says. "I feel like part of a family when I pray. I don't have to worry about how much I have messed up."

Arron doodles with his pencil. "When I burn the sage, I alternate between saying 'God have mercy,' and 'Thank you Creator.' Something releases me when I think about every day as a new day."

"How do you do this in your traditional practices?" I ask.

After several comments, Drew sums it up. "We take the time to look at our own feelings of being out of balance. Then we do something in our tradition that symbolizes walking in beauty, like sitting in silence inhaling the sage. With that we return to wholeness and start over again."

Leaning forward, I ask, "Does it always work?"

Drew answers, "I think wanting to get rid of the black hole within us and accepting ourselves as complete puts us in a spot where we can accept starting over again. If I try to take the easy way out I just disintegrate."

This gets several nods and we sit in silence. Finally, we say goodbye and go our separate ways.

As we talk, I consider the many elements in our journey to become whole. We mess up. We realize that being broken hurts and keeps us from looking honestly at ourselves. We want to be a part of that which gives us energy and makes us complete. And above all, we claim a new day, starting with no past garbage.

This takes practice. Wholeness can come unbidden. Or we can invite it.

Sacred Path 15: Going to the Center

Some mornings I rise with sticky ashes in my mouth, regretting or hurting about something that has happened.

So, what holy practice do I use that moves me through such murky circumstances and back into the light to live in beauty?

Sometimes it is prayer. Or I remove myself to a contrasting environment, or recall good times or give thanks or… But what happens when I cannot get beyond the terribleness of what has happened; when I am so off balance that I cannot think through anything?

I ask the Native youth.

The clown of our group, Sammy, takes charge. "Let's go to the Grand Canyon and get connected with the dirt."

Three people volunteer to take the drive the next Saturday. We stop at a little used viewing site.

"What exactly do we do?" I shift my body around, a little uncomfortable that I don't know.

Danny looks at the ravens swooping in the sky. "This is something we do when we don't feel connected to anything important. That's why you left your camera and laptop in the van. We sit on Mother Earth and look at Father Sky."

Lifting the sacred objects out of his grandfather's box, he sprinkles the corn pollen in four directions and gives us each a pinch to taste and pat on ourselves. Rafe lights the white sage in a sea shell and smudges us. Then we sit down under the tree and put our hands on the dirt. We don't talk. We just sit. Small sounds surround us with the rustle in the leaves and the birds swooping down.

At first my mind will not let go of all the negative vibes inside me. Finally, I breathe in the scents from the trees, feel every bump from the ground. Something loosens in me. The dirt takes hold. The sky beckons as the ravens fly overhead. I don't know how long we sit there. Eventually my center returns. We look at each other and get up to leave.

As we get into the van, we decide to get something to drink. I feel like I am floating on a distant cloud.

At the café we drink some ice tea and talk about being reconnected this way. We enjoy the outside benches where we can gaze over the Grand Canyon.

"Usually I just go outside and sit on the roof," reflects Sammy. "That's when I need some silence and some outside time. Afterwards, I feel like I have been reconstructed inside out."

Danny looks at the ravens flying overhead. "That's why I like to go back to the rez to visit my grandparents. I can be outside whenever I like. Sometimes I just have to sit on the ground under a tree."

We drive home mainly in silence. Of all the blessings I have received from the Native youth, this goes to the top of the list. As the years pass, it has become harder for me to get up from the ground. But it is so worth it to go outside and sit on the dirt in silence.

Being able to center yourself and then return surrounded by Mother Earth is a thing of beauty.

TOBY: A Personal Story of a Native Sacred Path

I saw a cat run over when walking home. It made a pitiful sound. I ain't no St. Francis but I carried the little limp body home where I wrapped it up in my shirt and dripped some milk in her mouth. She limps now but curls up on my lap when I sit down. I couldn't just leave her on the street to die. My grandfather taught me to respect everything from Mother Earth as our kin.

It's funny but I used to be a scrapper looking for a fight. I would mellow out with pot if stressed and never face anything. If I got caught, I never had to stay long in juvie. I thought things went my way until we headed to Skid Road in Los Angeles.

I didn't want to hand out food and juice to homeless dudes but I went with the others in our youth group. I kept touching my ear and fidgeting until my homie asks "What up with you, Bro?"

With a dry mouth I admitted, "I don't feel easy here."

"Nothing to it," he says. He turns to a couple of men sitting on their sleeping bags against the wall. "Hey, we got extra. You want some sandwiches?"

Before I can take a breath we plop down to eat with the men and talk about sport teams. We laugh and argue just like my brothers sitting on our sofa. They start asking what I do. I tell them and they shake their heads.

"Hey man, you've got to get it together. No glory in being a pothead. You got to learn stuff and get a job. Don't end up like us."

They go on like that, which gets to me. My body starts getting heavy and I let out my breath slowly. I nod but can't get words out. We wave goodbye. I pull my ball cap lower on my face and sort of angle away from my buddy. I don't want anyone to talk at me.

Well, that did it for me. I take a long walk after that and sort through just who I want to be. I realize that I can do a lot of things that I wrote off earlier because I thought I was stupid or lazy or something damaged.

When we hold our group's reflection on the day, I speak from my heart for the first time. "Man, I saw the holy today. I met some unwashed angels who spoke to me hardcore and I heard it."

Nobody laughs and we all talk about how different things look when we meet people who turn out to be good inside. "You know, good like someone with a warm smile that is real and whose body relaxes when he sees you."

More and more good things keep popping up. My store manager greets me like a brother. My classmates peer over my shoulder and help me with math when I get stuck. I even have a rug for my living room floor.

The Holy lives where good takes root. I even see it in myself now.

Mission Trip, L.A., CA

APPENDIX
ADDITIONAL CURRICULUM USED BY SPIRIT JOURNEY YOUTH

To survive and advance in our technological world, we use skills to maneuver both the social environment and the spiritual domain. For these Native youth, learning how to participate in a larger social environment and finding encouragement in the spiritual domain can heal generational wounds.

These following general basic steps can be used to teach any skill.

a. Give a context for how this skill can benefit the youth.

b. Hand out the procedures or write on board.

c. Go through each section by having the group give an example or giving one yourself for clarity.

d. Give them a set amount of time to complete the exercise. If they get stuck, give additional examples and explanations. Each exercise may take more than one session to finish.

e. When everyone is finished, ask for comments. It's okay if no one wants to share.

f. Reflect on exercise:

> **1.** Which question was most surprising? Most difficult? Easiest? Most helpful?
>
> **2.** What did you learn about yourself from this exercise?
>
> **3.** How might you become different after using this skill?
>
> **4.** What is your next step?

SECTION ONE

Three Exercises for Social Environment

To be functional in any society, an individual has to see him/herself with a vital role.

> **Employability**: to be self-sufficient in our economy by recognizing and using physical and human resources.
>
> **Civil Participation**: to take part in issues found in your family, local community, work, nation and globe.
>
> **Cultural Story**: to be able to sculpt meaning and identity through profound stories.

Employability Exercise

Employable Skills
List the work skills in which you have ability.

Work Experience
List your previous jobs, volunteer work, chores, summer employment.

Relationships
How do you adapt your style with an abusive boss, with unreliable peers, with customers? How do you cope with crisis, unexpected or unreasonable demands?

Education
List schools attended, degrees, certificates, other training or special courses.

Work Values
List qualities important in the following:

- job completion
- diversity
- teamwork
- punctuality
- initiative

Interests/Goals
What are your short and long term goals? What type of work inspires you—outdoors, indoors, methodical, open-ended, teams, individual, etc.? What do you see yourself doing in five years?

Underlying Questions
Are you willing: to work in uncomfortable situations in order to learn a skill? To follow a work dress code? To approach your job with energy and enthusiasm?

CIVIL PARTICIPATION

In many ways, citizenship is a foreign concept to those who have been marginalized. Often they do not vote or join in discussions of issues beyond their families. Often I hear "Why bother? Nothing I say counts anyway."

The lack of participation in the political dimension keeps the disadvantaged from influencing how their lives are governed or even if the street in front of their house can be paved.

Issue Awareness Exercise

Give an example of issues that influence your quality of life. Include issues from family, work, community, nation and world.

1. How do you want things to be different?
2. How will these changes be beneficial?
3. What are the possible disadvantages?
4. What authority or system can make this change?
5. How will you invest your time/self in this change?

CULTURAL STORY

Human dignity demands meaning and a sense of belonging. Often when a clash occurs with the minority culture of the youth, they would say something like "I don't fit on the reservation or in the town. No one values me whatever I do."

Cultural Story Exercise, Part 1

1. What values did you learn as a child in your own culture? What was important? What did you get scolded for? Rewarded for?

2. List values that begin with "Don't forget…" "Always remember…" Especially those values concerning integrity, respect, kin, strangers, possessions, creation, thankfulness and religion.

3. Which stories do you remember as a child?

4. Who did you want to be like? What qualities did you see in that person?

5. Name common clashes or misunderstandings you have when interacting with other cultures?

6. What values do you dislike in the majority culture?

7. What values do you have for surviving in a culture that is different?

8. Name the values you admire in the majority culture.

Cultural Story Exercise, Part 2

What do you want your grandchildren to remember about you?

1. I am known as

2. My friends know this about me.

3. I will never forget…always remember…

4. As a child I learned these things were important.
5. As an adult, I keep these things as basic to my identity.
6. I want others to see these values as important to me.
7. My purpose in living has these elements.
8. The stories I want my children/grandchildren to remember about me include…

SECTION TWO

Three Exercises in the Spiritual Domain

To be transformed means that a person finds the strength within to take advantage of whatever happens. It involves having the right attitude to find opportunities.

To hope is to have external stories, metaphors, and symbols for internal victories.

The harsher the external environment the more crucial it becomes for the individual to access deep inner resources.

The methods we use to journey as spiritual people include meditation, prayer, and contemplation.

> **Meditation**: To be in active dialogue with those writings and people who communicate profound wisdom.
>
> **Prayer**: To hold up concerns to wholeness and light.
>
> **Contemplation**: To become aware of the continuous presence of the holy.

MEDITATION

We live in an information age where excessive data overwhelms us. Meditation is an exercise of finding meaning through the eyes of faith. Following is one of the formats we use.

Meditation Exercise

Sample Quote:	Bishop Steve Charleston "I am not giving up. No matter how crazy it gets, how grim or goofy. I signed on to hope a long time ago and I am not going to give up on it now."
Basic Data	Which words or phrases stand out in this reading?
Associations	What experiences do I associate with it? What emotions are triggered?
Values	Which values can be seen through it? How is it important?
Significance	How does it help me see the sacred in ordinary things?

PRAYER

The spiritual practice of prayer involves going inside to focus on concerns. It is not a manipulative practice to get or achieve something, but a way to hold up your cares in profound wholeness. Without prayer, our concerns turn into random anxieties.

Prayer Exercise for Beginners. Begin in Silence.

Title	To whom do you pray? Great Spirit, Grandfather God, Holy Lord, That which is…
Concern	What or for whom are you lifting up concerns? Anxieties, people, desires?
So That	What do I want to happen? So that I may see, so that they may be whole,…
Name of	In whose name do you pray? In the name of Christ, of all names of the Holy, etc.

Sample prayer:

>God of our ancestors,
>We pray for street people who are ignored and abused
>That they may know they are worthy of respect
>In the name of Mother Earth.

CONTEMPLATION

Contemplation means to focus within yourself in silence and rest in total acceptance of the given situation.

Often there is a prelude to contemplation. Anything that disassociates you from your routine can enable you to enter into contemplative rest. You may let your senses carry you into stillness. Examples can involve smelling sage, watching a candle, listening to a muted bell, staring into a fire, watching clouds, smelling grass, or feeling dirt under your feet.

Contemplation leads us to accept rather than try to fix things. There is a freedom when we do not have to say anything, do anything, or be anyone. When we contemplate, things get sorted out on an unconscious level, deep in our soul leaving us restful.

The practice of contemplation takes many forms in the Native ceremonies. Silence is always the main component. The prelude often consists of chants, drums, sage, fasting, pipe, flute, sweats or running to the sun.

Contemplation Exercise

Prelude	Sprinkle corn pollen in four sacred directions. Then burn sage and bless each person.
Stance	Sit on the earth and breathe in smells around you
Contemplation	Sit in silence for twenty minutes or longer until you experience stillness within.
Ending	Walk away silently

Prayer from the Episcopal Hip-Hop Prayer Book

Used for Daily Worship

"No matter where you from Or where you at

He down for you He got your back

Heal you and forgive your sins

Not just one or two but all of them

Repent you in hell Even if you a thug

Hes got no grudge All He has is love.

Break it down, now."

Pacific Ocean, L.A., CA

CPSIA information can be obtained
at www.ICGtesting.com
Printed in the USA
BVOW11s1809070517
483062BV00006B/35/P

9 780692 846797